Guidelines for Spiritual Direction

by *Carolyn Gratton, Ph.D.*

Studies in Formative Spirituality: Volume Three

General Editors:

Adrian van Kaam, C.S.Sp., Ph.D.
Susan Annette Muto, Ph.D.

Dimension Books · Denville, New Jersey

STUDIES IN FORMATIVE SPIRITUALITY

General Editors:

Adrian van Kaam, C.S.Sp., Ph.D.
Susan Annette Muto, Ph.D.

Volume One: In the Midst of Winter
                by Louise Hageman, O.P.

Volume Two: Spirituality and the Desert Experience
                by Charles Cummings, O.C.S.O.

Volume Three: Guidelines for Spiritual Direction
                by Carolyn Gratton, Ph.D.

First Edition Published by
Dimension Books, Inc.
Denville, New Jersey

Nihil Obstat: Rev. William J. Winter, S.T.D.
                Censor Librorum

Imprimatur: Most Rev. Vincent M. Leonard, D.D.
                Bishop of Pittsburgh

May 15, 1980

L.C.C.C. No. 80-68087
ISBN O-87193-130-3

TABLE OF CONTENTS

                                                              Page
General Introduction.   9

Foreword   15

  I. INTRODUCTION
      The search begins.   21

 II. EARLIEST CHRISTIAN SPIRITUAL DIRECTION
      Jesus as spiritual director.   27
      The mystery in the early Church   33
      All direction centered in Christ   37
      The baptismal experience   43
      Early spiritual Fathers   45
      Finding the connections   49

III. THE STRUCTURE OF GUIDANCE SITUATIONS
      Among the people of God   51
      Guidance in the contemporary world.   53
      Our society as milieu of all guidance situations.   55
      Lack of freedom in our society   58
      Experiences leading people to seek guidance   60

 IV. WHAT SPIRITUAL DIRECTION IS NOT
      Current expectations of guidance.   66
      The psychotherapy or counseling situation   69
      Movements towards religious counseling   73
      The pastoral counseling movement   77

  V. A NATURAL FOUNDATION FOR SPIRITUAL
     DIRECTION
      Human desire for the Real.   81
      Changing goals of therapy   83
      The shift towards meditative presence   84
      Reflective living and therapy   87
      Faith as the context of spiritual direction   90

VI. SPIRITUAL DIRECTION OF CHRISTIANS
     The source of spiritual direction 95
     An example of transformed perception 98
     The part played by experience 101
     Connection of baptism with mission 106
     Self-knowledge in spiritual direction 108

VII. THE PARTICULAR INDIVIDUAL WHO COMES
     Basically healthy and free........................ 111
     Socially conditioned and defensive............... 117
     Lacking a sense of self-identity 120
     Tending towards illusion and encapsulation 125
     Having problems with interpersonal relations 132
     Distorting the meaning of the other.............. 136

VIII. THE PERSON FROM A SPIRITUAL POINT OF VIEW
     Spirit in flesh 143
     Called and free to respond...................... 147
     Defensive and resisting......................... 152
     Sinful yet loved 156
     Lost in substitutions for God.................... 161
     Saved by the Spirit 167

IX. PRESENCE OF THE THERAPIST
     Influential personal presence 171
     Unacknowledged perceptual limitations........... 173
     Limitations of psychotherapeutic presence......... 177
     Ways of evoking the other...................... 182
     Need for self-knowledge........................ 185

X. THE CHRISTIAN SPIRITUAL DIRECTOR
     Primarily concerned for the Kingdom 188
     Needing a holistic image........................ 190
     Lacking a revealed view of the person............ 194
     The practice of disciplined presence.............. 196
     A mature channel for God's love in the world 199

     FOOTNOTES 204

ACKNOWLEDGEMENTS

I am grateful to my students, clients and friends in Pittsburgh whose lived interest in the relationship between spiritual direction and therapeutic counseling encouraged me to write this book. To Father Adrian van Kaam whose insights into formative direction have been an inspiration for many years and to my colleagues at the Institute of Formative Spirituality, Dr. Susan Muto and Dr. Charles Maes, a special debt of gratitude is owed. Also to my family in Toronto and to friends in the Grail in different parts of the world, a sincere thank you for loving support and for sharing so freely questions that emerged from direction-seeking hearts.

GENERAL INTRODUCTION

The Christian today has entered a new era in the formation history of humanity, characterized by rapid transition. The time of a monolithic Church that formed civilization exclusively is behind us. The Christian enclaves that succeeded the break-up of medieval Europe will not return either. The ghettoes have broken open and we are exposed to other directives and forms of life. Faced as we are by a bewildering number of options, it seems difficult to relate them to our life direction in Christ, who is the Divine Form and Image of our soul.

In a world of increasingly complex formation directives, we find ourselves often confused about how to give form to our life call in the Lord. The secular world is dynamic, fascinating, seductive. Beguiled as we are by its projects, we may allow our life to be formed according to its enthusiasms rather than growing as Christ-directed people in accordance with divine inspirations. We become so adept at reacting that we forget how to respond out of an inner at-oneness with the Lord and His word. We try to adopt new styles of life, to be in with what is current. We define ourselves mainly on the basis of our occupations and hobbies, or on how our neighbors value us. We become our secular roles to gain the approval of the world. The problem is that we may betray the image of Christ in us that should penetrate and transfigure these roles. We take on new patterns of living, yet we do not try to harmonize these with our Christian values. We slide along thoughtlessly, bewitched by the media, seduced by the sophistication of our secular peers.

Propelled by our aspiration to give form to our lives, in tune with the times, we forge ahead, often in directions that have no real meaning for us because they are at odds with our inner divine direction. We lose our concrete sense of a life call, communal and unique. The more lost we become, the more desperately we search for substitutes. In our desire to live meaningfully, we may rush after any fad that offers a quick solution to this spiritual quest.

While present day secular society is a confusion of life forms and styles, it offers at the same time an astonishing variety of incarnational possibilities. It enables Christian formation to express itself in a richness of empirical forms undreamt of before. Because of this pluralism of life forms, more types of Christians can express their unique foundational form of life within the limits of their community commitments. They can find their place in the Father's house where those many rooms promised by Jesus are now becoming manifest. We may have lost security and conformity but we have gained creativity and pluriformity. The uniform Christian culture may be dead, but Christianity itself as a source of formative wisdom is more alive than ever.

Since it is no longer sustained by a universal Christian culture, Christianity is like a leaven spreading itself through the dough of a redeemed humanity, transfiguring countless cultural styles and forms with the words and wisdom of Christ, incarnating itself in myriad ways in this modern world. Creative formation of life in Christ has become a much more personal responsibility. The secular society offers no guidelines for the authentic formation of the Christian life. Only Christ and His church and the masters of the spiritual life, who lived in His light, tell us what is involved in spiritual formation in dialogue with the ever-changing world where He calls us to be His "little flock."

The purpose of this series of books within the science of Foundational Formative Spirituality is to contribute to this dialogue. The publications in this series will direct themselves to various dynamics of Christian formation, illuminated for us in scripture and tradition, that gain in depth of meaning when placed in dialogue with emerging insights in literature, human sciences, and contemporary experience. Each study intends to help the reader find his or her life form in this unsteady age. Each intends to help us answer such basic questions as: how can I find my way as a creative Christian in the new, wide open situation of a diaspora Christianity? How can I live the formative message of the faith in a unique yet communal style now that there is no longer a uniform cultural code to tell all people in minute detail how to incarnate Christ in their life and world?

Christian formation can be seen as a discipline that guides this search for our communal and unique form of life. The words of scripture, the teaching of the Church and its spiritual masters, illumine this pursuit. They inspire attitudes and formative dispositions enabling us to be more open to the Christ-form within us. Formative Spirituality explores these attitudes; it examines how we prepare for them, how they transform our daily life. When spirituality is approached in this practical way, it is called Formative Spirituality.

The focus of the formative approach is on the conditions, structures, and dynamics of Christian unfolding in daily life. It wants to facilitate the graced disclosure and unfolding of our divine destiny. This new field of study tries to establish the necessary and sufficient conditions for our spiritual formation. It examines from this perspective special and personal ways of formation, experiences, devotions and exercises, abstracting in this way the essentials. It attempts to provide the Christian with a lasting foundation for graced formation in Christ. It assists him or her in finding practical and particular solutions to the formation questions one will have to face without betraying the fundamental conditions of Christian formation.

This approach also takes into account the psychological, social and physiological obstacles that may interfere with the disclosure of our human and graced life direction. Similar obstacles may hinder the full permeation of our life by this disclosed direction. The human sciences contain findings and insights regarding such obstacles. They suggest effective ways of coping with them. Formative spirituality integrates — and, if necessary, transforms and reformulates — such insights along with those found in Church doctrine, scripture, spiritual theology and philosophy into a synthetic understanding of the spiritual formation of the Christian.

Formative spirituality is in this way profoundly practical, for it refers to what effects a real change in the inner life of the Christian, one that will affect in turn his formation of the world in concrete ways. Change of a superficial nature affects mainly the emotional, psychological or external surface of human life; profound change effects a lasting inner conversion reverberating in one's practical formation of the world. Formative spirituality tries, therefore, to disclose, describe and apply the principles of the process of a profoundly practical change by grace. In this way it wants to be of help to Christians who go through conversion or transition crises at various successive stages of a deepening of their life by grace and nature.

Formative spirituality builds on a theory of the development of human life in relation to the invitation of grace. Contributions from such fields as the biblical and historical study of spiritual formation, the critical-textual approach to spiritual masters, and the systematic theology of spirituality are taken into account whenever advisable or necessary. They are, however, not the primary focus of this new field, which is to assist Christians in the disclosure and unfolding of an empirical, communal and unique life form rooted in their human make-up and in the direction the Christ-form in their soul gives to their lives.

During the past eighteen years of developing this specialty, the results have been most gratifying. The vast majority of students, after study and preparation in this field, have reported spontaneously on profound changes they experience in their own life and in that of people entrusted to their care. The studies presented in this series have been written by men and women who for a prolonged period of time have participated in the unfolding of this new discipline at the Institute of Formative Spirituality at Duquesne University. It is our hope that this series will enable the reader to participate in the fruits of this new field of study and to become more aware of the formative dialogue and deepening to which each Christian is called.

The Editors

FOREWORD

By Adrian van Kaam, C.S.Sp.

The third book of our series of Studies in Formative Spirituality is on formative direction. It complements in a superb way the two former books in this series on suffering and on the desert experience, for the questions and doubts engendered by the pain of suffering and the loneliness of the desert make us seek direction for our lives.

The foreword of each book of this series is not meant to simply praise and summarize its excellent content. The purpose of this introduction is to suggest how such content can be related to the overall theory of Foundational Formative Spirituality and of this series of studies in this field in which it appears as a valued contribution. Dr. Gratton's book is indeed an asset to this series, rich in ideas and suggestions that we will not repeat here so that the readers can discover and enjoy them for themselves. Our aim is to place this important study into the total picture of the science of formation and of its emergent expression in this series.

The subject of this study by Dr. Gratton is "the heart that seeks direction." In this science of formation, the human heart plays a central role. Formation is an expression of the foundational form or "soul-image" of Christ in the depths of our being. Christian formation tries to give concrete form in day to day life to this "soul image." Our empirical life is basically formed by the affects of our heart, for the heart is the integrative center of the feelings that move and direct us. Our heart, however, should be enlightened by the wise appraisals of our mind under the guidance of the Holy Spirit. These graced directives should gradually transform the heart in such a way that it becomes a harmonious core of affective inclinations drawing us toward the human and Christian formation of our own life, that of others and the world.

The enlightened heart should safeguard the congeniality of our life direction with the foundational Christ-form in our soul. At moments of crisis and transition, of suffering and loneliness, we may become aware that we need a basic change of heart. We receive new messages that have to be appraised for their formative meaning. They may lead to a new disclosure of the unique foundational life form of our soul. At such moments we may feel the need for formative direction. Such direction is usually thought of as being private and personal. However, formative spirituality tries to rekindle also an interest in what it calls "formative direction in common." Direction in common, as the phrase indicates, is a direction given to more than one person by means of the spoken or written word in scripture, liturgy, spiritual writings and sermons, and in formative direction sessions.

Formative direction in common is in some form available to all Christians. Private direction is generally less available and may entail complications that arise easily in an intimate one-to-one relationship. The guiding question in formative direction should be: in what way can this direction foster or hinder the disclosure, unfolding and implementation of Christ's direction of our life by the formation of our heart.

The central means of formative direction in common is formative-inspirational teaching. We say *central means* because the communications of the teaching director shared by all may be complemented at times by dialogue with his audience and by periodic personal contacts with individual persons who participate in the direction sessions. Formative direction should increase and deepen the faithfulness of our hearts to our life call. The implicit reference point of all formative direction is the divine direction and formation of redeemed humanity. The unique direction of our heart within this overall divine direction particularizes itself via a unique appeal heard within the deepest recesses of our heart. From this same center grows the directee's response to the divine direction that draws him. God's mysterious ways of directing and forming people may thus include His use of a director who reached people privately or in common by means of the written or spoken word. What matters most here is that the directee remain open in the center of himself to what the words of the director mean for him in light of his own life direction.

One prevalent danger disclosed by formative spirituality in relation to direction is that of introspection. Hence the development in our science of the distinction between introspective and transcendent self-presence. (See Adrian van Kaam, *In Search of Spiritual Identity,* Denville, N.J.: Dimension Books, 1975, Chapter VII). Introspective reflection tends to be analytical and aggressive. In introspective reflection, we isolate the "reflected upon," such as guilt and shame, from the larger backdrop of reality. We not only cut the "reflected upon" off from the larger whole to which it pertains; we also cut it up in its inner wholeness. For example, we do not put a failure in our formation in the perspective of God's all-encompassing providence and forgiveness. We engage instead in a fragmenting analysis of every aspect of our experience of deformation.

Introspective reflection implies a focusing process in which the background of our formation is either blurred or lost. We lose sight of the totality and try to force insight aggressive analysis or by digging up all we can recall of the past. While this approach is excellent for analytical pursuit, it is destructive for any kind of transcendent reflection that aims at the integrative formation of our life as a whole.

What I term "transcendent reflection" or "transcendent self-presence" is the opposite of introspection. In it we may reflect upon ourselves, others and nature to become one with a Divine Source, mysteriously made whole in an Eternal Origin. We may reflect meditatively upon the divine mystery of formation, its flow and simplicity out of which all forms emerge. In such transcendent presence we do not leave the formative presence of the merciful Source of all formation. We relate the ultimate meaning of our formation problem to this Divine Origin. This reflection is not divisive but unitive; it is transcendent; it makes whole; it attunes us to a formation mystery by which we are already embraced. It is a healing reflection. Far from being dissective and aggressive, it is meditative and gentle, a gentle preservation of all formation events as allowed and as tenderly held in the splendor of a Divine Presence. It is a source of patient spiritual formation. Whenever formative direction helps us to reflect upon our life in this meditative way, I call such reflection "transcendent self-presence."

Dr. Carolyn Gratton has taken up these and many other themes originally formulated in and developed by the science of foundational formative spirituality as taught by us for many years at the Institute. In accordance with some of the principles of the research methodology of this new field, she explored what Christian tradition teaches about spiritual direction. Another methodological principle of this science, concerning the dialogue between Christian formation tradition and the relevant findings of the human sciences, has led her to consider, among other things, the relationship between spiritual direction and therapeutic counseling.

We are grateful that Dr. Gratton, a faculty member of the Institute, took the time and energy to research and write on such an important topic as spiritual direction, illustrating and expanding different concepts of the science of formative spirituality.

Suffering, desert experience, and now direction of the human heart are not the only themes that are relevant to spiritual formation. Other books, forthcoming in this series will highlight other aspects of Christian formation. They will be based on the same principles of the science of formation that made the first three books of this series so relevant to people in search of their communal and unique life form in Christ.

January, 1980
Duquesne University

CHAPTER I

INTRODUCTION

The search begins

These chapters on finding the connections between contemporary psychology and traditional spiritual direction originated as nine separate papers prepared for groups of men and women interested in the work of spiritual guidance and formation. It often happens that psychologists working in the field of spirituality become aware of the light psychological insights can shed on questions of a spiritual nature. However, it was practical questions emerging from the lived experience of the people in these groups that prompted me to prepare talks and later to write about how the two disciplines relate to one another.

Only a few of these people were trained as professional theologians or psychologists. Not all called themselves Christian, although most did. Many initially were suspicious of words like "spiritual" (illusory? floating? removed from the here and now?) and "direction" (hierarchical? authoritarian? lacking mutuality?). All were straightforward people sincerely interested in discovering the practical implications of current psychological theory in service of the particular guidance task they were involved in.

Each chapter echoes the practical experience of these searching people — their insights, questions and problems. They suspected, and rightly so, that there is a significant difference between apparently similar guidance situations, such as the therapy encounter, and what has traditionally been called Christian spiritual direction. They wanted to be able to distinguish between the psychosocial approach of the former and the "spiritual" meaning of the latter. They also wanted to appreciate their interconnectedness, and to see how the one discipline could enlighten and complement the other. They were unwilling to perceive their own and others' experience of needing guidance in the midst of life's concrete limitations and problems as separate from the Gospel injunction to become a spiritual person. They were convinced that a clinical psychologist could add something to the understanding of their task.

As our sharing unfolded against the background of the Christian mystery, the scope of our search necessarily widened to include many aspects of the 2,000 year-old tradition of Christian spiritual guidance — the "care of souls" as it was once called. [1] We were obliged to recognize the contribution of the great masters of the spiritual life from all ages and stages of the tradition. Moreover, since we were interested in an incarnational spirituality, we could not overlook its more situated aspects. Thus, we tried to root our discussions in the reality of today's life, seeing how "direction" is embedded in the actual people, events and things of daily existence. Methods of appraisal or discernment also were examined, as was our own reflective consciousness of the motivation of daily decisions and actions. Our life of prayer as a source of "direction" came up for consideration, especially in relation to the Church's yearly cycle of liturgical feasts and fasts and to our sacramental participation in that life.

At a certain point we realized that the time had come to begin collecting some of this material into an orderly form. A decision was made to begin at the beginning, looking at our own and others' actual experience of what it means to be a guide in both the psychological and the spiritual sense. We went back to the primitive structures, to a "bare bones" analysis of guidance situations in general. From there we moved, as recorded in Chapter III, to consider positive and negative experiences that ordinarily lead people in our society to seek out some kind of new direction for their lives. Simultaneously with seeing the contemporary reality of guidance in all its variety and lack of true freedom, the groups consulted the Gospels and the Epistles for broad guidelines as to how the first Christians were helped in their search for a meaningful existence. We were interested in the heritage Jesus left his followers by way of aim, method, preparation, content and approach to their personal and communal search for "direction" in the New Age. We found that "spiritual" freedom for him always involved the person's concrete situation. His method of spiritual direction brought about a shift in the whole person, completely transforming his or her attentiveness to the hidden directives of the Kingdom "already there" beneath the obviousness of daily life.

Thus, Chapter II with its brief biblical description of Jesus as spiritual guide sets forth the basic framework in which the connections are to be sought. Focusing on how the Mystery was perceived by the early Church and on Baptism as the connecting link between everyday experience and the revelation of its mysterious ground, this chapter describes an approach to guidance that is truly spiritual and at the same time acceptable to us who must search for our direction now, twenty centuries after Christ came to reveal it.

In the years between these earliest Christian beginnings and our time, spiritual guidance has undergone a complex series of shifts in method, content and direction. Others have traced that history in detail.[2] For us, it is more to the point to begin where we find ourselves at the present moment, surrounded by the bewildering variety of self-transformation techniques and spiritual paths presented to us by our culture. We need to confront "what spiritual direction is not" before moving too easily into assumptions about what it is. Chapter IV invites us to survey elements of three apparently similar but nevertheless fundamentally different current directional possibilities: the psychotherapy or counseling situation; various religious counseling movements, and pastoral counseling. We are given an opportunity to distinguish them for ourselves by observing some of their structural differences.

Chapter V, in its incorporation of recent interest in traditional Eastern as well as current psychological techniques of meditation, encourages us to appreciate the contribution such knowledge can make to our emerging understanding of spiritual direction. We see that the graced life of faith finds its foundation in our natural human capacity for inner awakening and development. We also move closer to an understanding of faith in the mystery of Christ as being the ground or context that distinguishes and gives identity to the process of explicitly Christian spiritual direction. Chapter VI attempts to deal with resulting confusion about the aim and type of transformation peculiar to spiritual direction as distinguished from the above-mentioned types of guidance. It also introduces the part played by everyday experience in that transformation, and points to the place of self-knowledge and active ministry in the spiritual direction of Christians.

The next two chapters are devoted to articulating theoretical images of the human person who comes seeking either psychological guidance or spiritual direction. Chapter VII makes use of terminology and concepts peculiar to secular psychological movements in bringing forward a positive view of the human person as regards basic health, freedom, social conditioning and defensiveness.

Brief descriptions of the origins of normal neurotic patterns, of anxiety and lack of self-identity, of tendencies towards living in illusion and encapsulation and of problems that arise in human relations as a result of innate tendencies to distort the meaning of the other person, are of use to the spiritual guide despite the absence of customary "spiritual" language. It is hoped that readers will understand the author's reluctance in this and other chapters to add still another language complication by consistently using both masculine and feminine pronouns. It was tried and found to be impossible in writing this book.

With Chapter VIII we find connections between the person seen as "situated freedom" and the scriptural approach to the person as "incarnated spirit." We also discover something new here — the revealed truth about human persons and their graced destiny. This new spiritual image of the person completely transforms the meanings given to both the positive and the negative patterns and tendencies mentioned in the previous chapter. In the light of this understanding, our focus shifts to the freely choosing human heart. Now spiritual anxiety, sin, idolatrous worship of false gods, guilt and the meaning of one's unique "direction" become central. The differences in underlying assumptions and dynamics that exist between spiritual direction and counseling or psychotherapy emerge, along with the necessity of grounding spiritual direction in a deeply Christian view of the human person.

By this time there was more than enough material for a sizeable book. We realized, however, that in concentrating on the "now", we had barely touched the riches of the Christian tradition; we had said nothing about the centrality of motivation and its appraisal, or the potential directives to be discovered in events and situations of everyday life and in the life of the Church. The best solution seemed to be to bring these reflections on the connection between contemporary psychology and traditional spiritual direction to a close with two final chapters linking psychological understanding of the therapist's work to the unique task of the Christian spiritual director, and to look forward to future opportunities to work out the other topics. Thus Chapter IX indicates how liberation from unacknowledged perceptual limitations and growth in self-awareness can be as crucial for the spiritual director as for the counselor or therapist. Chapter X focuses on the preparation and spiritual maturity needed by any man or woman called to be a friend, guide, teacher or spiritual director of those who want to follow Jesus. In so doing, it completes this stage of our search by pointing to transformation of heart as the central goal of those who seek Christian spiritual direction.

CHAPTER II

EARLIEST CHRISTIAN SPIRITUAL DIRECTION

Jesus as spiritual director

If we really seek to understand something of the essence of spiritual direction, we need to pay attention to how Jesus himself went about it. He both reveals the directedness of all humanity towards intimacy with God and guides us into that relationship of love. We can begin by looking at the Gospels to see how he prepared for this task. What major themes comprised the content of the direction he gave? How was he present to his directees? What in particular characterized the method of direction he used? Starting from the first event of Jesus' adult life, his baptism,[1] we see the "beloved Son of God" being taken possession of by the Holy Spirit. He then goes into the desert to prepare himself to follow the Father's direction of his mission. On returning from the desert "in the power of the Spirit," according to Mark, he appeared in Galilee proclaiming the Good News that the Kingdom of God is at hand.

His major themes for the people who crowded around him were that they should reform their lives, believe, undergo a *metanoia,* become different and trust in the Gospel. The whole thrust of his message seems to have been in the direction of joy and liberation. From that time on, those who received the message underwent transformation into a new way of seeing their lives — they became a new creation. They were aware of the first creation; now a new one was being offered.

The following paraphrase of this directive by a contemporary writer highlights what must have been the expectation of a person in the crowd who had really grasped the type of direction Jesus was offering:

The time is ripe. The new age, the kingdom of heaven, is upon you now. Repent, and let a new consciousness dawn within you — let there be a change of heart and mind and will, so that you come to understand differently, feel differently, desire differently, choose differently.[2]

Already we begin to grasp something of the element of newness that pervades Jesus' spiritual direction.

The crowds came seeking this man, choosing him as their guide or leader. So many came that at times he had to teach them from a boat on the water. He taught them mainly by means of parables or stories. However, even when speaking to a large crowd, we see that he always sought to address each one personally, saying "Let everyone heed what he hears."[3] Each one who listened became personally responsible for what they heard, for what they saw, for what he had to give them. Jesus was not simply giving the same message for everyone. He was addressing the unique destiny of each listener. Not an arouser of the masses, he preferred to interest a few. So often, after he had given a parable to the whole multitude, he took a few aside and said he would explain it to them in particular; that he wanted them to understand away from the crowd.[4] What he was doing in these dialogues, when teaching or giving spiritual direction, was basically revealing what had been until that moment a hidden mystery. Jesus was the one who knew and who revealed the hidden meaning in the stories he told. For some the meaning of the parables remained hidden; they simply went away.

The Gospel accounts also tell us something about Jesus' method of spiritual direction. He often made use of dialogue. For instance, he asks such questions as: Who do people say that the Son of Man is? And who do you say that I am?[5] In asking such questions, he did not intend, as Socrates did, to expose error and confusion of thought. Rather, the people who were questioned in this way by him found themselves undergoing an inner change of some sort, for instance, in the direction of repentance or of commitment to the Kingdom. We notice also that Jesus did not have to publish a book or pass out flyers or even draw pictures. He simply spoke with people, asked them some questions, engaged them in conversation. Sometimes he got an astonishing response. Take Peter's declaration of faith when asked who Jesus really was. Peter was the only one who glimpsed the real truth at that moment, and he apparently grew in his own faith when he announced, "You are the Messiah."[6] In understanding something of the mystery of Jesus, Peter underwent a transformation.

Another person, this time one who asked Jesus a question, was the rich young man.[7] He asked specifically for direction. He wanted to know "What must I do to share in everlasting life?" It is clear from the exchange that he had amassed a fair amount of worldly security already, and we gather that he had some spiritual security as well. He had known and kept all the commandments from his youth; throughout his life he had done all the right things. He may have been feeling a little self-righteous at this point. In any case, Jesus looked at him with love. Mark tells us that there was a change in this person's perception, in his way of seeing after Jesus told him the one thing more that he must do — sell his possessions and give to the poor and follow him. A transformation took place. The young man's face fell and he went away sad, for he had many possessions.[8] A *metanoia* did happen to this well thought of, respectable young man. Perhaps the change was an indication of who he most deeply was. In any case, we are left wondering about the direction of his life from that time on.

Look also at Zacchaeus.[9] He seems to have come from the other end of the social scale, a tax-collector, not respectable at all. He had probably done a fair amount of cheating in his day. In fact, one commentator says that one could call him a "cutthroat" or "traitor."[10] Yet look at what happened to Zacchaeus in his dialogue with Jesus. He also changed his direction. Although the accounts do not mention this, when Christ saw him up in the sycamore tree, he probably looked on him with love. Everything then changed in Zacchaeus' life. He hurried down and welcomed Jesus to his house. He underwent a total *metanoia* in the liberating presence of the Lord. Jesus told him that this day salvation had come to his house, for this was what it meant to be a son of Abraham. The Son of Man had come to save that which was lost.[11] Obviously he was delighted to see the change that had come over his new friend. So we see that this method of personal dialogue used by Jesus consisted of speaking with someone in a loving, accepting way that brought about a change. Yet nothing could be guaranteed. After speaking with Jesus, one person went away sad while another entered the Kingdom.

When persons come to us asking for direction, we cannot know for certain what is going to happen. Each person obviously needs particularized guidance. Take, for example, the man in Mark's Gospel from whom the demon had been cast out.[12] The Lord told him to go back home to his family rather than follow him. Evidently not everyone who felt called to follow him was allowed to do so. Jesus' direction or guidance is particularized and situated, depending on who comes, what they are like and what their circumstances are. He does not make one rule for everybody — one mass proclamation of the Kingdom. He even sees spiritual qualities in those who were not of his own people. Mark tells us how he acknowledged the faith of the Canaanite woman[13] and of all kinds of others, and Matthew and Luke both record his words to the centurian: "I have never found this much faith in Israel."[14] People as diverse as Nicodemus and the Samaritan woman discover different messages in their dialogue with Jesus. Some words are healing for body and soul, others foster spiritual renewal and repose.

Two main points emerge from this descriptive consideration of Jesus as spiritual guide or director. The first is that when Jesus had a conversation either with a group, like the crowd who came to hear the parables, or with some of the above named individuals, he always took their situation into account while bringing about a life change, a change of heart. Something always happens: people are changed as a result of their conversation with him. Spiritual direction, as Jesus does it, is really a kind of liberation for the person; it involves a *metanoia,* a new creation.

The second point is that Jesus is interested in bringing this change about by means of a new and deeper kind of seeing and hearing. The Mystery is hidden; it needs to be seen and heard in a new way, in a way that people perhaps have not experienced before. The changes in attitude that are needed in order to penetrate the Mystery are an integral part of spiritual direction. After the resurrection the apostles understood. They saw that the "secret," the Mystery, has to do with a whole new order of being, with the order of grace that changes our nature so that we share the divine nature as children of God. This is what Jesus came to reveal as the new spiritual direction for everybody. It means a total re-orientation of life towards a new goal. It means that the will of God, the "secret plan," [15] the life of grace, the fact that we are God's children is the hidden direction of the entire cosmos.

As we begin to understand this spiritual direction, we may feel as did the apostles to whom Jesus said:

" To you has been given a knowledge of the mysteries of the reign of God, but it has not been given to the others. To the man who has more, more will be given until he grows rich; the man who has not, will lose what little he has. I use parables when I speak to them because they look but do not see, they listen but do not hear or understand. Isaiah's prophecy is fulfilled in them which says: 'Listen as you will, you shall not understand, look intently as you will, you shall not see. Sluggish indeed is this people's heart. They have scarcely heard with their ears, they have firmly closed their eyes; otherwise they might see with their eyes, and hear with their ears, and understand with their hearts, and turn back to me, and I should heal them.' But blest are your eyes because they see and blest are your ears because they hear. I assure you, many a prophet and many a saint longed to see what you see but did not see it, and hear what you hear but did not hear it. Mark well then, the parable of the sower." [16]

It has been noted by more than one scripture scholar that the directive to "mark well," to pay special attention to this parable of the sower, is used only this one time by Jesus. Certainly an understanding of this parable is important for anyone interested in directing others in the new spiritual attitudes appropriate for receiving the mystery of grace and the Kingdom that Jesus came to reveal.

The mystery in the early Church

Both St. John and St. Paul have much to tell us about the way the earliest Christians saw spiritual reality in light of their experience of being baptized into Christ, of being changed, of encountering the Mystery. Their perception, expressing as it does the world view of the undivided Church is, after all, the foundation of what we now call spiritual direction.[17] If we look at how they saw the event of Christ's reality in their lives and how that event transformed their view of the whole of history, we find first of all that for believers this history was seen as emerging in three stages. First there had been the time of the Old Covenant, from the beginning of history as recorded in Genesis through the unfolding of creation until a disaster called the Fall, a moment in which all of creation lost its integrity and unity in a major dislocation. After the Fall they saw a new eon or time recorded in the Old Testament. In the midst of this second stage an event happened that changed everything — a revelation of God projected into history. This second eon received its focus from one central event, the brief span of Christ's life on earth, his Incarnation, his Passion, his Resurrection. From that moment history continued to unfold in a totally different way.

Once people understood the meaning of this event and saw the unfolding of creation in terms of it, history became a kind of "between time," the time between the catastrophic event of the Fall and the regeneration at the end of time when the Son of Man will come again and initiate the third eon, the Parousia. It is this regeneration that Paul referers to in the Epistle to the Romans where he speaks of all creation eagerly awaiting the revelation of the Sons of God.[18] During this "between time," metanoia must take place for everyone. Transformation is to involve not only human beings; all of creation is to be directed towards the newness of regeneration. This then is the time of the Church, of the Christian community, of the possibility of metanoia through the preaching of the Gospel, and the revelation of the Mystery for all created beings. It is the time of the full revelation of the hitherto hidden mystery, the time of the New Covenant of love between God and persons.

We see in the primitive Church a lived awareness of the centrality of Christ glorified and ascended and now working in history through the Spirit. The early Christians perceived the between time as that of the Church sustained by the Holy Spirit in expectation of the return of Christ at the beginning of the third and final eon of history. Before the coming of Christ, such a view of history would not have been possible. We notice in his epistles that Paul is speaking not only to the expectation and the excitement of the end times, nor merely to the ideal of communal sharing of goods nor to attempts to love one another engendered by this view of the way things are heading. He is also speaking to points of discipline and to the need for guidance in day to day living that he found among the Christians in the early Church. In his Epistle to the Corinthians, he stresses the need for such guidance not only in relation to the eschaton, but also in regard to the present moral dilemmas in which people who wanted to follow Christ found themselves. They needed spiritual guidance not only in relation to the mystery in the mystical sense but also in the moral sense, one following from the other. This guidance as we see it in Acts and in the Epistle to the Romans was by way of group guidance, of mutual guidance of one another. People did not seek out one spiritual director but together as Church they seem to have been responsible for one another. This aspect of mutuality is seen clearly in the responsibility that the whole community took for the initiation of people into the central mystery of Baptism.[19] Such responsibility would seem to presuppose a real spiritual availability on the part of the faithful for mutual help, criticism and encouragement. For them, the life of faith was not something apart; rather it permeated their everyday relations with one another.

What were they trying to accomplish via this daily spiritual responsibility for one another? What was the hidden mystery that was to be transformative of their everyday lives? A careful reading of the New Testament uncovers an invisible yet taken-for-granted life direction that was pointing somewhere, that indicated a movement or flow both of history as a whole and of people's individual histories. This directedness is oriented by a hidden mystery that can only be perceived with eyes of faith in a risen Lord. The perceiver must have undergone that transformation, that metanoia, in order to recognize the hidden direction of all that is. In this regard, we read how the first Christians had to move from the experience that Christ was given over to death and all their hopes were shattered, to the experience that he had been raised by God and had sent his Spirit to be with them.[20] This change involved a complete overturning of the establishment of his Kingdom on earth according to any merely human expectations or plans. The new divine plan was centered in the resurrection; it illuminated the meaning of Christ's death, though it was only with the sending of the Spirit, that they were given real understanding of that death and of the resulting new meaning of the whole of history.

In Peter's discourse immediately after the descent of the Holy Spirit,[21] he notes that what the prophet Joel had prophecied in the Old Testament is being fulfilled. God is pouring out his Spirit through the death of Jesus, whom they killed and whom God has raised up. He continued, "This is the Jesus God has raised up, and we are his witnesses. Exalted at God's right hand, he first received the promised Holy Spirit from the Father, then poured this Spirit out on us."[22] In order even to begin to penetrate this mysterious direction, the hidden mystery, human beings need respectfully to approach the Trinity, the Father, Son and Holy Spirit working together. Understanding spiritual direction must include the three Persons of the Trinity and their mysterious inter-relationship. Peter continued, "Therefore let the whole house of Israel know beyond any doubt that God has made both Lord and Messiah this Jesus whom you crucified."[23] In response to their request for guidance, "What are we to do?", Peter then answers, "You must reform and be baptized, each one of you in the name of Jesus Christ." Here the familiar themes emerge again: change, metanoia, reform, turning around of life and ideas followed by baptism in the name of Jesus Christ into a totally new design or way of life.

Evidently Jesus' death is a necessary aspect of that plan, of the saving design of God. This is the way God chooses in order that he may pour out the Spirit on all people. Not only is this what God continues to do throughout all of human history, it is also how he has decided to do it. So the Spirit of Jesus is available, is "already there" before anyone starts what we would call "doing spiritual direction." We on our part must tune in to this hidden reality, this mystery that underlies everyday life, trusting in the central mystery of Christ and the power of his name. It is this power, this name of Jesus as Lord, that is the source of energy for living in the time between the resurrection and the regeneration, the eon which is our time and the time of spiritual direction.

All direction centered in Christ

All aspects of primitive Christian life, community of goods, oneness of heart and mind, communal prayer and Eucharistic meal were part of this transformation, as the early Christians grew in their perception of the new reality brought about by the new Adam. Paul's famous parallels of the old and the new Adam, of sin, death and evil contrasted with liberation through the life of grace, of the natural body versus the spiritual body, of the earthly Adam and the heavenly Adam, come to mind here. His Epistle to the Romans speaks of the contrast between the life of the whole human person as "flesh" and the life of that same whole human person as "spirit."[24] Paul locates the metanoia moment in the turning from one way of being in the world to the other. He addresses the early Christians as actually being "in the Spirit" since the poured out Spirit of God dwells in them. Thus, he can say that anyone who does not have the Spirit of Christ does not belong to Christ. But (and notice here is the secret, the hidden mystery) if Christ is in you, the body is indeed dead because of sin, while the spirit, the pneuma, the interior life is alive. "If the Spirit of him who raised Jesus from the dead dwells in you, then he who raised Christ from the dead will bring your mortal bodies to life also through his Spirit dwelling in you."[25] Here we have a first description of the aim of spiritual direction, the spiritualization, the permeation or penetration of our mortal bodies, our vital, functional, personal, social selves by his Spirit dwelling in us.[26] In other words, Paul is saying that if people cooperate with the gift and find the spiritual direction of their lives, they will be allowing the mystery of Christ dwelling in them to be revealed, to inform the whole of their existence.

It is important to see this entire plan of salvation in terms of the gift of the Spirit in Christ, in terms of Christ's dwelling in persons, for we find here the concept of our being the body of Christ, the adopted children of God. "All who are led by the Spirit of God are sons of God. You did not receive a spirit of slavery leading you back into fear, but a spirit of adoption through which we cry out "Abba," (that is, "Father"). The Spirit himself gives witness with our spirit that we are children of God."[27] So for Paul as for Jesus, it is this divine adoption into the mystery, the possibility of sharing life with the Trinity, that constitutes the original directedness of everyone. He also repeats a concept of change or metanoia held by Jesus when he says, "The Lord is the Spirit, and where the Spirit of the Lord is, there is freedom."[28] That freedom is freedom from guilt and death, the courage to act and love, to live in peace, justice, joy, hope, in short, the fruits of the Spirit. He continues, "All of us gazing on the Lord's glory with unveiled faces are being transformed [that is, are undergoing metanoia, are being changed] from glory to glory into his very image by the Lord who is the Spirit."[29] This adoption really means a change into being the very image of God.[30] This is the ultimate possibility of the human person, a hidden possibility in each one which is the deepest meaning of who we are. Paul cautions the Corinthians not to lose heart because, contrary to their somewhat opposite external experience, this inner being is renewed each day. He adds, "We do not fix our gaze on what is seen but on what in unseen. What is seen is transitory; what is unseen lasts forever."[31] He seems to be suggesting that what we need is a conversion to the spiritual dimension of reality so that we will undergo a change in perception and be able to perceive more of the invisible reality than we have approached so far.

In the Epistle to the Romans, we find a progression from the necessity of belief in Christ crucified as the principle of transformation[32] to the concrete meaning of the Christian life, the new life that comes from the Spirit, particularly in Baptism. Paul describes it as living under grace rather than the law.[33] Then he reminds us of how this new life involves a real tension because we are still under the law and we still must recognize our sinfulness, our identity as sinners in need of forgiveness. We can identify with Paul's description of the human condition, knowing that the law is spiritual but recognizing ourselves as weak flesh sold into the law of sin, and then having to admit, "I cannot even understand my own actions. I do not do what I want to do, but what I hate."[34] We human beings have had glimpses of the mystery. We see that it would be really fine to live that way, but somehow we cannot seem to manage it. With Paul, "I know that no good dwells in me, that is, in my flesh; the desire to do right is there but not the power."[35] Here he points to the deepest intentional self that exists in every human person, a self that has already said a somewhat weak but sincere "yes," and yet cannot carry out its desire on the level of action. It is to this state of affairs that we must refer when we are involved in spiritual direction. Otherwise impossible demands may be made if there is failure to recognize how things really are for both persons involved. Everyone finds him or herself doing "not the good I will do, but the evil I do not intend," repeating wryly with Paul, "What a wretched person I am! Who can free me from this body under the power of death? . . . So with my mind I serve the law of God but with my flesh the law of sin."[36] This is how it is, living after the Fall. No one of us is able to love and keep the commandments without the help of grace. This is surely one of the more primary realities to be recognized by all who approach the task of spiritual direction.

Paul goes on to point out that the law of the Spirit in Christ has delivered us from the law of sin and death, from the law which can only reveal the tragedy of carnal man and the power of sin in him. The new law and the pouring out of the Holy Spirit does not abolish the human condition but fulfills it in grace. And where do we find this saving wisdom, this deepest mystery that consists in the revelation of a divine secret? We find it hidden like a treasure in a field, that is discoverable by those Paul calls the "spiritually mature" to whom God has revealed it. He says, "What we utter is God's wisdom: a mysterious, a hidden wisdom. God planned it before all ages for our glory. None of the rulers of this age knew the mystery; if they had known it, they would never have crucified the Lord of glory. Of this wisdom it is written: "Eye has not seen, ear has not heard, nor has it so much as dawned on man what God has prepared for those who love him."[37] This is the wisdom that is fruit of contemplation. It is the kind of knowledge that Paul wanted the early Christians to have. He is speaking of what can be expected of the average Christian when he continues, "Yet God has revealed this wisdom to us through the Spirit. The Spirit scrutinizes all matters, even the deep things of God."[38]

We can conclude from this that although God has revealed this wisdom, a mystery like the in-dwelling of the spirit of Christ cannot be known except through the Spirit of God. Paul is telling us that we cannot figure out this type of wisdom or knowledge for ourselves, nor can we reveal this deep directedness to another person unless the Spirit is helping the person's heart to understand these depths of God in his or her life. Thus, "the Spirit we have received is not the world's spirit but God's Spirit helping us to recognize the gifts he has given us."[39] Evidently this recognition involves discovering what is "already there," and perhaps, as Paul indicates in the next verse, interpreting spiritual things in the spiritual terms in which they are revealed. He points out that the natural man does not accept what is taught by the Spirit of God. So the uniqueness of the process of recognition or appraisal must be based on natural man's inability or the inability of unaided human cleverness to recognize what really is. "For him that is absurdity. We cannot come to know such teaching because it must be appraised in a spiritual way."[40] It should not surprise anyone, then, that spiritual direction also, unless it is carried out in an atmosphere of faith under the guidance of the Spirit of God, will sound absurd to those who have no contact with the mind of Christ, for he is the center and source of all spiritual direction.

In John's Gospel there are many parallels to this attempted description of the mystery. John himself had a long experience of life in the "between time" before he wrote his version of the meaning of the early Christian experience. In trying to reveal the hidden plan of God to the Church, he spoke to the people's need to be reminded of the dynamics of the invisible directedness of all that is at a time when the visible reality of their history seemed, in the age of the martyrs, to be so contradictory. He testifies to the invisible light of glory shining in and behind even the visible darkness of Christ's crucifixion and death. In his Gospel he tries to show Jesus as he really is and as he enters into glory by way of darkness and tribulation. John too wants to point out the hidden mystery of the adoption of all humankind into the life of the Trinity, and the blindness that prevents us from recognizing the light even when it is in our midst. Thus, perception in a transformed mode is thematic in his Gospel too, as God's initiative in Christ enters the lives and hearts of those who are open to it and they see a new directedness of all that is, towards the Father's enduring love. According to John, it is Jesus, the only one who really knows the Father, who now makes him known to us by renewing our minds so that we can recognize the one whom Jesus presents to us, for if we "see" Jesus, we actually do "see" the invisible Father, because Jesus himself *is* the perfect revelation of God.

Besides the conflict between light and darkness, we find that central to John's Gospel is the theme of baptism, the entry into the light of this new life. In Chapter 3 we find Nicodemus asking about life and baptism, and being told that both visible water and invisible spirit are needed in order to enter into a life of glory. John could be reminding listeners assembled at an early liturgy of the invisible glory that accompanies the tribulation of this life and of the fact that the initiative for this glory is God's. Christian life then, as now, is nourished by the Eucharist and the Spirit gives life to the flesh. Faith involves that radical transformation of perception that gives us the ability to see and understand something of this invisible reality that inheres in the visible. In his first letter, John reiterates this understanding of the divine plan when he says: "See what love the Father has bestowed on us in letting us be called children of God! Yet that is what we are. The reason the world does not recognize us is that it never recognized the Son. Dearly beloved, we are God's children now."[41] What he is saying here is simply that anyone who has been baptized has already been radically transformed. Yet there is much that still needs to happen. Growth has to take place, and "what we shall be later has not yet come to light." However, he continues, "We know that when it comes to light [that is, when it becomes visible, when we can perceive itl] we shall be like him [that is, transformed on an ontological level into his image] for we shall see him as he is."

In other words, our perception will have undergone such a total transformation that we will be able to perceive in a way that has hitherto been impossible for us. The direction, the meaning of this whole metanoia in John's Gospel, lies in our becoming able to love, in our being motivated by love, in our becoming, as he expresses it to the Samaritan woman, a "fountain of living water" for others.[42] This, then, is where the spiritual director has to start, at the frame of mind suggested by John as he remembers to tell us that Jesus loved the rich young man before he challenged him to change the direction of his life. It is God's initiative of love that is the foundation on which all spiritual direction builds.

The baptismal experience

One way of speaking about the aim of spiritual direction is to say that it attempts to uncover the "already there" initiative of God's love in the life of the person. This loving initiative implants the divine life in us at our Baptism. Baptism is the foundational reality for people who are interested in spiritual direction, because the aim of such direction is the gradual permeation of more and more of our being by the divine life given at Baptism. In Mark's Gospel we find several parables relating particularly to the idea of the growth of the seed, to the fact that " the seed sprouts and grows without [our] knowing how it happens."[43] For Mark, the Christian is someone whose faith in that planted seed grows and develops, without the person himself experiencing much of the process. In Baptism we see a parallel in that the experiential realization of the mystery does not happen all at once. Particularly those of us who were baptized as infants would agree that a baptized person does not feel very different simply because he or she has been baptized. In his Epistle to the Ephesians,

Paul claims that God has given us the wisdom to understand fully the mystery, the "plan he was pleased to decree in Christ"[44] which begins in its fullness for each person at the moment of his being baptized. But that realization comes slowly in actual experience. One must grow into a gradual realization of what has happened, of the new life that is actually there.

The seed is there, but there are also many barriers to a trusting faith in the seed's growth. Psychological blocks and mental hang-ups and long held habitual ways of being and doing, prevent us from recognizing who we really are. Christians need to let the realization of the event of being baptized move out of the mind and into the heart, into our whole being. We have to try to understand Baptism, but we need still more to unite ourselves with its graced effects in us, to become one with the seed hidden in the field that is ourselves. In discovering that treasure we need to draw our minds into our hearts and discover there the working of the Holy Spirit in faith that the seed which was sown there is good and will produce good fruit because that seed is Christ. Letting God be God in us to this extent is the way the metanoia will be brought about.

The early Christians saw Baptism as the turning point of their lives. They recognized in this one event many others — faith in the Risen Christ, metanoia or conversion of heart, renunciation of Satan and experience of the Holy Spirit, who can show us the hidden things of God by teaching us a new way of seeing. In the Epistle to the Corinthians, we find an account of the contemplative knowledge of the things of God that the people seemed more or less to take for granted. Through the Spirit they were familiar with the "deep things of God,"[45] with his indwelling in each of them. There seems to have been a contemplative access to this whole world of meaning for these baptized adults. They seem to have glimpsed something of the wonder of the glorious mystery that permeated their life together, to have had a realization of God's personal love for each member of their community. They did not live merely out of blind obedience to an impersonal magisterium; rather their sharing and their love for one another came out of a real experience of the wonder of the riches of God's gift to them personally. They were people who had allowed Christ to transform them from darkness to light. In fact, such a change was part of their conscious expectation at Baptism.

Perhaps contemporary spiritual directors should be equally expectant of change as a result of the baptismal grace that is the "already there" mysterious foundation of the life of those who come to them. Such an expectation would rest on explicit faith in one's mystical baptismal entry into the whole reality of Christ's death and resurrection. This is the change that belongs to spiritual direction — a change or transformation that is utterly beyond our human capacity to bring about. This transformation has its source in the life of Christ and the Holy Spirit working in each particular baptized person.

Early spiritual Fathers[46]

Having considered the scriptural rooting of spiritual direction, let us turn briefly to the early Eastern tradition to see a concrete example of this art as it appears in the first centuries of the Church's life. From the point of view of the early Fathers of the Church, we can get some idea of how people acted as spiritual directors in the more formal sense. The way such men as St. Anthony of Egypt directed people spiritually resembles closely the way Christ went about it.[47] When these men are called "Abba" this title refers to the fact that they were considered to be persons who did not simply pass on ideas about the spiritual life, but truly "fathered" children in the faith. To these children they passed on a heritage of abundant life, of a richness that encompassed the whole person, and informed the heart as well as the mind about what it means to be a Christian. St. Anthony was a man who went deeper and deeper into the desert in order to pursue his own journey to the Father. Jesus too, at his baptism, having come from the desert, was confirmed or shown forth as the beloved Son of the Father. Divine sonship, though not the same as that of Jesus, is the gift to all who are baptized, including saints like Anthony. The spiritual father in the Eastern tradition is seen as someone who can help others on the journey to the Father because he himself has gone further along that road of union. As he journeys, people seek him out somewhat in the same way that Christ was sought out by the crowds in Galilee. In fact, one of the reasons these desert fathers went into the desert in the first place was precisely to get away from the crowds. We recall that Jesus also had to retire to lonely places in order to pray, in order to have time to be with his Father.

The desert father is someone who by long experience in the solitude of the desert has learned something of the secrets of the spiritual journey, something more about the human capacity for deeper seeing of the hidden mystery. By "secrets" we do not mean the gnostic sense of an elite kind of knowing unavailable to others, but rather the secrets that become available to anyone who undertakes this particular journey into intimacy with the Lord. It is also interesting to note that the desert fathers were not priests. The monastic movement for the most part was a lay movement whose members chose to spend their lives intent on the task of finding their own spiritual direction, their own destiny and relation with the Father first of all. In their case, it is clear that the director as well as the one who came for direction was personally involved in discovering, discerning and deepening in the mystery. As time went on, we see that the direction given by one monk to a single other person had to change, as monasticism became a systematic way of life for many. Guidance was given to these larger groups as the directives of the spiritual father were written down for all to profit by. Yet always the spiritual father was there to help them individually. General rules, as we have seen from the guidance given by Jesus, always need to be interpreted for particular individual persons. One general rule can never adequately discover the will of God for all persons in a group, because there are always particular cases. In this regard, we have already seen that Jesus, after giving general directives, also took care to speak to persons as unique individuals.

In Orthodox Christianity the spiritual father or "starets" was a charismatic figure. He was chosen for his task by the Holy Spirit, so that the initiative for his calling came not from a human source, but from God. An orthodox spiritual director is never self-appointed. Others approach him and ask to be under his spiritual care, somewhat in the same way that the crowds sought out Jesus. At the moment when he no longer sends these people away but accepts their coming to him as a sign of the will of God, the spiritual father allows himself to be revealed to himself as a "starets" by his spiritual children. But this choice is preceded by a time of preparation that points to a somewhat classic pattern. We see this pattern in the life of Anthony of Egypt, who spent the first half of his life in ever increasing seclusion in the desert, and the second half available to others who broke into his solitude and demanded that he become their spiritual father. Anthony did not withdraw in order to become a spiritual master or guide for others. He wanted only to be alone with God, who accepted his love and then sent him back as an instrument of healing in the world. He undertook first of all his own metanoia, his own spiritual journey in order to become transformed himself into a certain kind of presence. His flight would have been valuable to society even if he had never returned, because he did the most important thing first. He helped the world not primarily by what he did or said but by what he was. It was his invisible in--touchness with God that made his visible service to others bear fruit. He established himself in God and then was able to bring others to His presence. Anthony's very presence became a healing one for others, a life-giving presence for those who were hungry for life.

One writer,[48] in speaking of the conversion of heart that must be undergone by one who becomes a "starets," describes the career of teaching, preaching and pastoral counseling typical of the contemporary spiritual guide who may be too busy to have taken much time out for dwelling in the creative silence of the desert. He notes that in the midst of all the busyness of teaching, we ourselves may slowly begin to learn, and to recognize our powerlessness to heal the wounds of humanity solely through philanthropic programs, common sense and psychiatry. Our complacency is broken down, we appreciate our own inadequacy and start to understand what Christ meant about the "one thing only that is required."[49] That is the moment, claims the writer, when we enter upon the path of the "starets." It is through our pastoral experience, through the anguish and pain of those we would help, that we are brought to undertake the journey inwards, to ascend the secret ladder of the Kingdom, where alone a genuine solution to the world's problems can be found. He adds that although few of us would think of ourselves as a "starets" in the full sense, we can all share to some degree in the grace of being a spiritual parent, provided we seek with humble sincerity to enter into the "secret chamber" of our heart. He seems to be saying that it is only "hermits of the heart" who will be able to understand the secret, the revealed mystery that makes up the hidden core of the spiritual journey. It is only those who have undergone some type of preparation whose perception will be cleansed and transformed so that they can "see" differently.

Finding the connections

When the early Christians listened to the memoirs of the apostles being read during their assembly on the first day of the week, they could have made some interesting connections between what was being read and the actual experience of members of this first generation of their community. From the readings they, like ourselves, could also learn much about the art of spiritual direction. For example, in John's account of his and Andrew's first meeting with Jesus,[50] we find the two of them standing with their spiritual director, John the Baptist. Having undergone his own time of preparation in the desert, John the Baptist is ready to recognize the divine Sonship of Jesus when the Spirit descends on him at the Jordan. Awake to the secret hidden in the Old Testament revelation, he had made the connection. This is the Lamb of God who would take away the sin of the world. When the crowds sought him out, choosing him as their spiritual director, this humble friend of the bridegroom knows that it is not himself but

Jesus, the Messiah whom they seek. Attentive to Jesus, he tells his two directees that this person is the Lamb for whom the generations have been longing. From that time on, when people come to him hungry for life, he turns them in the direction of the Source of life now in their midst. The directees leave him. He has pointed them in the direction of the hidden mystery — the mystery of Jesus' dwelling in the Trinity.

As spiritual director, John the Baptist's context is the whole of revelation, the apocalyptic message of the Kingdom of God. Yet Luke also tells us that his call for conversion and his announcement of the creative moment was particularized by specific directives for different individuals.[51] He is aware that the Spirit will begin working in these people's lives in mysterious and unpredictable ways, and that all he, John, can do is to indicate to them where the Source of this life is to be found. The community, listening to this account, familiar as they were with the Old Testament prophecies, would have made the same scriptural connections as did John. As recent converts, they knew from personal experience that seekers for life would find it by following Jesus. In dialogue with the one who already knew the deepest desire of their hearts, they have been changed, brought to a new "seeing," a new attitude towards reality — an attitude called faith. The spiritual direction given by John the Baptist and continued by the earliest followers of Christ will always center on life — on a lived relationship; on introducing others to the possibility of abiding or dwelling in the fullness of life that Jesus came to reveal; on finding the connections between our life in this world and the good news of the Kingdom.

CHAPTER III

THE STRUCTURE OF GUIDANCE SITUATIONS

Among the people of God

When we look closely at situations in which people came to Jesus for spiritual direction, we see that sometimes they came in crowds and he opened the Mystery to them in sermons and parables; other times individual persons came asking for direction, like the rich young man and Zacchaeus, Nicodemus and the Samaritan woman. It seems that each time people came to Jesus they experienced some sort of change in their lives. In loving dialogue with one or several of them, Jesus revealed as much of the Mystery as they could handle at that moment. He helped them to perceive, with new eyes, the invisible meanings that he himself embodied.

Christian life itself emerged as a growth in perception and an experiential realization of the implications of the event of Baptism on the whole of one's human life precisely because these early Christians understood their initiation into the Mystery as their being caught up into an invisible divine plan centered in Christ. Also, because they had ventured further into the mysterious journey to the Father that Jesus had come to make available for everyone, the early Fathers of the desert were sought out by people as spiritual directors or "Abbas." Some later formed communities of such seekers under a general rule of life; others chose life styles more compatible with their life situation. Their example shows that throughout the centuries both crowds and individuals have tended to seek guidance from persons who have journeyed further into the Mystery and who seem to embody an invisible meaning that is "more than" what is offered by the visible reality the seekers are presently experiencing.

Taking into account these basic principles, let us look now at what we might call the "bare bones" of any contemporary spiritual guidance situation, keeping in mind the incident from Mark's Gospel of Jesus and the rich young man and John's account of Jesus' spiritual discourse to the crowd about the bread of life.[1] Towards the end of this chapter we will lay aside the specifically Christian aspects of these early guidance situations in order to discover the essential elements of the guidance situation in general. Then we will begin to be able to understand better the guidance that is specifically Christian, i.e., Christian spiritual direction.

From the above mentioned accounts in the Gospels of Mark and John we see that guidance, like any other human situation, takes place in a shared world of space and time. In both of these cases, we are inserted into the first century social milieu of Palestine at a particular moment of its history. At least two, perhaps more people come together and are present to each other in a more or less reflective and influential way, just as Jesus was present to the rich young man and the hungry crowd. Something happens in the exchange or dialogue "between" them; one or more of the people is inwardly different after the encounter. The young man was "sad" and the crowd was "shaken"; he went away and the people murmured and protested. In a spiritual guidance situation, therefore, we note a coming together of several lived worlds of meaning.[2] This coming together can be experienced either as a harmonious flowing union or as a clashing collision of these worlds, or as a mixture of both. The world of Jesus and the lived worlds of the majority of that crowd really clashed, so it seems, since most of them went away angry; up to a certain point at least, his world of meaning and that of the young man seemed to flow parallel.

Actually, the participants in a spiritual guidance situation usually make each other be, or call each other forth, primarily in an affirmative way on the level of spirit. Even so, the experience is not always a comfortable one. Although to all appearances the people are sharing a similar visible world of commonly understood social meanings, their reflective exchange, because it draws them deeper into the underlying reality, may disclose different inner worlds, different levels of experience, and an unsuspected variety in their horizons of value. Yet it is precisely within this disclosure of values, within this process of finding what the other actively cherishes, that the seekers' hearts are drawn towards or away from the invisible Mystery that is being disclosed. It is here in a concrete specified space/time meeting of people that the "something" we call spiritual guidance can happen.

Guidance in the contemporary world

There are many situations in contemporary society where one or more persons come together like this. Colleagues settle down for a chat; a teacher lectures to a class; best friends explore each others' worlds; a consultant presents his or her values to an audience; a therapist speaks with a client; a guru inspires his disciples. These people share a common twentieth century world of space and time. In their reflective presence to each other they disclose some cherished values. Their exchange inevitably throws light on the world of lived meaning each one is, even when they attempt to color or conceal that world in order to avoid clashes like those referred to above. We need to distinguish still further these apparently similar human experiences, to clarify which ones actually are situations of spiritual guidance or direction. To reach the full meaning of such a situation, then, we must go beneath what appears to be happening in the mere surface behavior or activity of the people coming together to talk and listen to each other. We need to be aware not only of the exchange of values between them, the happening or "figure," but also of the "ground" or context against which it takes place.[3]

Once we pay attention to the fact that no aspect of experience — no person, thing or event that we encounter in life — can be experienced without its accompanying ground or the invisible halo of meanings and relationships that are its context, we begin to recognize that each experience is distinct from the other, and yet there are ways in which each is connected. When I meet someone, I am conscious that both I and the other bring to that encounter previous worlds of relationship and experience, expectations, hopes and fears. Meanings and confusions trail behind each of us like a comet's tail. Sometimes these invisible worlds of meaning and value flow together in harmony; we agree, we like each other; we feel content to be together. At other times, often after we have moved to a more profound level of speaking, our worlds of meaning or certain aspects of them clash; we begin to disagree about almost every topic. As time passes and our values are further disclosed, we may discover that our first impression of agreement or disagreement was mistaken. This acquaintance, friend or teacher, speaker, therapist or guru was emerging from a ground rich in meaning and intentions that were never suspected at our first meeting. Both figure and ground were "already there" when we met, but it takes time for the latter to be perceived.

In the sixth chapter of John's Gospel, we can see precisely such a figure/ground pattern emerge. On the surface most of the crowd came seeking Jesus because of a visible value he offered them — free bread combined with the political possibility of a visible miracle-working leader or king. Yet for many the external quest for perishable food concealed an invisible desire for "more than" that, for a better life. The young man in Mark's Gospel may also have wanted "more than" a confirmation of his rather self-righteous record of doing all the proper things. Beyond his ego-functional complacency lurked the inevitable question, "Is that all there is to life?" The invisible ground of Jesus' life was such that he could offer to the crowd more than merely visible miracles and power, and to the young man more than the operative key to how one gained eternal life. Yet, because at the moment of loving dialogue the young man's understanding remained statically fixed on the original "respectable" level of his seeking, he missed the invitation to unheard of loving intimacy with the Father. Similarly most of the crowd also remained unchanged in their understanding of the spiritual values Jesus disclosed; their pragmatic worlds of meaning clashed with the deeper invisible horizons of spiritual nourishment and the life of grace and union with the Trinity that Jesus was offering them. Both they and the young man "went away" because the experience that had brought them to the one who embodied the invisible values they were seeking had not been accompanied by an openness to radical personal change.

Our society as milieu of all guidance situations

It is not only intentional personal worlds of meaning

that flow together or collide when two or more human beings encounter one another. The larger world, that is, the social reality with its problems, trends, customs and values is also always "already there" as context of every meeting. There is no way in which we can ignore the pervasive influence of our socio-economic condition, or for that matter, of the conditions that prevail in the world and national cultures. Even the ideological prejudices and fads of our immediate social milieu, with their accompanying lack of logic and irrationality, are an element in the invisible ground of our dialogue with the other.

Just as the people who came to Jesus trailed behind them a comet's tail of unconscious longing for "more," so too were they imbued with commonly held prejudices — not only against a "local boy" as poor as themselves, who claims to know more than the "home folks," but more seriously against a supposed teacher who seems to contradict tradition and whose ideas border on something as socially unacceptable as cannibalism. In our time too, no one comes for guidance outside of their current social milieu; everyone is marked by whatever the "in" prejudices for that year or decade may happen to be.

As cultural trends change and are reformulated, our identity as contemporary persons undergoes accompanying shifts in orientation. Since we are products of what has been described as an alienated, divided, pluralistic, class-conscious society, where anonymous typifications and depersonalized relationships prevail, and where at best people confront one another from initial stands of mistrust and defensiveness, we should not be surprised to find that this "shared world of meaning," whether we are aware of it or not, influences our being together with one another. We do not need to read too many descriptions of our North American social situation to recognize the extent to which the stresses and strains of contemporary societal conflicts and pressures, even when they have not reached pathological dimensions for the individuals concerned, can and do involve both teachers and students, gurus and disciples, speakers and audience, therapists and clients, as well as spiritual guides and those guided. One writer has called these phenomena "socioses."[4] Socioses are alienating patterns in our larger social situation that tend to make us sick, anxious and somewhat neurotic. They inevitably influence our seeking for guidance and our being able to understand and participate fully in the values that may be disclosed to us, especially if these values transcend the spiritual level of the society and culture in which we find ourselves.

In summary then, guidance situations in our twentieth century society consist of a constellation of two or more persons whose personal worlds of meaning engage each other against a backdrop of somewhat alienating socio-economic and cultural meanings and values. It is within this dynamic process of value disclosure between persons that guidance can be said to take place.[5] In contemporary North America, a guidance situation "gestalts" as such when people appreciating certain values decide to come together with other people, or perhaps with one other person, whose presence both embodies and discloses the values that the seekers would like to be living themselves. People seeking guidance may feel, for example, that the horizon of values presented for their lives by society in general is not enough, and that this other person, this guide, points to "more than" they have so far experienced. They believe that being in the presence of (talking to, telling their story to, listening to, arguing with) this other person (teacher, friend, guru, speaker, therapist) will help them inhabit their own world of meaning in a more satisfactory way; this meeting, in short, will help them grow and develop, will bring them peace, or whatever it is they seek. And so we find the crowds and individuals of our time also flocking to those who they feel embody and disclose values that are "more than" their present life experience seems to provide.

Lack of freedom in our society

The phenomenon of so many people seeking new orientation for their lives in our time brings into focus other elements that are also necessary aspects of guidance, especially of guidance on the level of the spirit. Although these elements belong to the realms of freedom, personal choice and interest that are proper to the individual, they are often as remote from the seeker's awareness as are the more "given" societal elements mentioned above. Yet every person who comes to another for guidance is already living in a world of given and chosen meanings — a hierarchy of ways of being that he cherishes and pays attention to, that he affirms and seeks to modify, or that he denies and/or would like to avoid or minimize. For instance, like some members of the crowd that came to Jesus some of us, from time to time, may be concentrating on the world of pleasure, bodily satisfaction, comfort. We may be intent on expanding this mode of being, and choose to be guided by courses in gourmet cooking, instruction on how to enjoy our leisure time or develop physical or sexual prowess. At other times we may choose to be guided in another direction, a more functional one. Then we will look for the guidance we seek among the hundreds of teachers, therapists, and even gurus in the culture who can help us work through the individual, social, functional and aesthetic aspects of growth. We will choose among a rich variety of behavioral, technical, vocational, informational, humanistically and artistically oriented workshops, schools, camps, and development centers. In a society like ours where humanistic and technological values flourish, it is not surprising that much guidance is to be found at these two levels, and within a more or less pragmatic horizon, since the persons doing the guiding also emerge from a similar value background.[6]

For the person interested in life on the spiritual level, all these possibilities offered by our society raise the question of where we can find the freedom necessary to move beyond the kinds of guidance that focus merely on the functional level of economic values, on techniques of competence and consumption, on modes of production and over-busyness. Is there not a danger that exclusive development along merely vital-functional lines only helps people to don more and better masks of specialization and expertise while at the same time they become even more embedded in securities that are false and life styles that are defensive and routine? A society that only provides guidance on the levels mentioned above would not be conducive to the ultimate freedom of the persons in it.

There have no doubt been persons in our society whose responsible sense of deeply human values has motivated them to challenge others beyond a merely pragmatic meaning horizon. In their concern for human meaning and destiny, figures from our past — philosophers, prophets and sages from the East as well as many great women and men from the West — have agreed on the need to transcend a purely immanent view of reality. Their values have outreached the idolatrous "little beyonds" that every one of us tends to substitute for the transcendent.[7] They have been the wise ones of the ages whose calm gaze uncovered the limitations not only of our absorption in personal and cultic allegiances, but of our cosmic illusions as well. Guides of such stature, however, are few and far between. It would seem that most of us in this century in North America continue to exist as divided selves in a divided society[8] that has settled for immanence, and in so doing, has repressed in us the possibilities for spiritual freedom, i.e., for a breakthrough to the also "already there" transcendent ground of our existence.[9] On the other hand, perhaps it is our experience of this very lack of freedom, this dividedness itself, that is the condition that impells people now, as it did in the time of Jesus, to seek out another for guidance towards something new.

Experiences leading people to seek guidance

Looking again at occasions of spiritual guidance as Jesus lived them we see, on the one hand, the crowds and the single individuals who are not satisfied with their lives as they are. They want to change somehow: the poor want to be less poor; the sick want to be well; sinners need to be forgiven; the mentally ill seek sanity; those who are not coping want to know what to do; those who want to grow spiritually ask for faith to perceive the newness Jesus offers. On the other hand we see Jesus, and later his followers, men like Peter, Paul and Anthony, who glimpsed something more of the Mystery; they are further along the way to the Father, and are able to share the hidden meaning or value that Jesus stood for. What the people who came to them for guidance experienced was personal attraction to a value embodied for them in a person, and at least an initial openness to be changed by or in relation to that value.

What about us in the twentieth century? What is the nature of the shift in a contemporary person's world of meaning that would lead him or her to seek out the reflective presence of another person, be it friend, teacher, therapist, counselor or guide, in order to explore the unsatisfactory nature of their lives and their felt need to change? What human experiences most commonly underly our need for guidance? What are the resources we have available to answer this need?

Instead of presuming that people today will automatically seek out Jesus or his followers in a spiritual search, let us leave aside all specifically Christian implications at this point and simply discuss the various types of guidance that the majority of people in secular society seem to see as responding to their search for change and/or guidance in a new direction. I shall point first to one kind of negative human experience that seems to be at the root of contemporary quests for guidance, and then move on to more positive experiences that can also impell modern people to seek out some sort of guide.

The negatively tinged experience I am referring to is one that accompanies moments or periods in life of not being able to function adequately, of being at a loss regarding what to *do,* of not being able to manage life as one has been accustomed to doing. I am not speaking here of those everyday occasions when some useful object or tool breaks down and we matter of factly call on an expert to repair it; or even about the more or less emergency situations when we call a friend for help because we have run out of time, money, energy, etc. I mean rather to look at the times when we experience a breakdown of our usual taken-for-granted ways of doing and being, a moment when we experience an inability to function, a split within ourselves, a moment when "ego desperation"[10] sets in and our managing pragmatic self can no longer flow with its world. In such moments, we may become conscious of a felt separation between the self and reality because we lose our accustomed control and are no longer "in touch" with our world.

This more or less conscious accompanying feeling of not being in touch, of not belonging, of not inhabiting well certain areas of our everyday world of meaning, can be an anxious one for people of our society especially. Finding themselves no longer at home with their bodies in a comfortable owning of sexuality and unself-conscious movement, no longer fruitful and productive in the everyday controlling and ordering of the universe, no longer at ease in their relationships with people and the larger social reality, they may seek relief from this impaired functioning by looking for someone who, at-home himself in these areas, can tell them how to move back into at-homeness themselves. Some thinkers describe the accompanying negative experiences in terms of neurotic or emotional problems. They speak of degrees of ego loss, fixation in infantile modes, inability to refrain from neurotic obsessive or hysterical patterns of behavior, impaired perception of reality, schizoid separation from reality, embeddedness in guilt, and failure to adjust. Others translate these anxiety-laden experiences of people, events and things into the language of functional achievement, and speak of failure to find the self, to attain one's goals, to reach fulfillment or self-actualization, to establish relationships and communication with others, to explore fully the self or the now-moment. However they are described, we find that often in our contemporary world, it is negative dichotomous experiences of this type that first lead people to recognize the need for personal change and impel them to seek out someone who will act as a change agent on their behalf.

The positive side of many of these seemingly negative experiences can also move one to undertake a search for change, newness, and transformation of life, for a person or group of persons who are further along than we ourselves are in living the transformed life style that seems most valuable to us. The moment of ego-desperation, of losing touch with one's capacity to function well, can shock people out of their embeddedness in the taken-for-granted world of pragmatic meanings and shift their recognition to a new perception of the way things actually are.

We know that every day human beings suffer losses of all kinds. We lose those dear to us; we are deprived of physical health; we suffer losses of self esteem, material security, friends and social relationships, of various familiar worlds of meaning. Depression so severe that we need to consult a therapist may be the result, but there is also the possibility that with the disappearance of one way of being in the world, and thus of perceiving its reality, another mode of being and seeing may take its place. In the course of working through an experience of loss or anxiety, we may be granted a momentary glimpse of what might be called an alternate reality. The immediately experienced situation does not change in such a moment; what changes is our experience of it. Our way of seeing it may be transformed, so that its "ground" opens up, revealing other dimensions that we are now invited to discover. Our consciousness has undergone a shift and we discover the "more" that was previously invisible. Then we recognize our need for a guide who is familiar with this wider view, someone who can direct us along the way to this "new seeing."

Even when life is experienced more on the positive end of the continuum, contemporary persons may still experience the urge to seek out some sort of guidance due to a consistent sense of dissatisfaction with the contrast between seemingly successful coping with the immediate realities of daily life and a lack of at-homeness in their overarching ground, the universe as a whole, or the Mystery of All That Is. Feeling restless with a life of mere satisfaction, suspecting that this is not "all there is,"[11] has certainly been a force impelling millions of middle class American women to find others who are asking the same questions and seeking a new direction in the woman's movement. Also, in spite of the absence of deep anxiety and fear, human beings from time to time experience a certain guilt for not living up to certain ontological demands that seem to come from beyond the sphere of their daily functioning. In this regard, too, we can look at the eagerness of people in our time for guidance in what has been called, among other things, the contemporary spiritual search, the search for meaning, the journey inwards, the search for self- awareness — all concerned with the process of inner discovery with its ensuing change and enlightment.

People are beginning to awaken to their own restlessness with mere satisfaction or are finding themselves in a negative, uncomfortable "place" in their life journey. In either case, unable to cope, or simply restless and dissatisfied, people today seek help from others. They look for someone who is already coping, who inhabits certain areas of reality more comfortably than they do, who can direct them in value realms with which they are relatively unfamiliar. They may or may not be aware of all the possibilities open to them at this particular time in history, but their pressing need for some kind of change or transformation in their existence prompts them to seek out the presence of a guide of some sort, be it friend, teacher, therapist, speaker or guru. What is important here is that the guides be able to distinguish among the possible options that come under the name of "guidance" in our time, and thus state clearly what kind of help they themselves are or are not able to offer.

CHAPTER IV

WHAT SPIRITUAL DIRECTION IS NOT

Current expectations of guidance

When a person decides that he or she "needs to talk to someone," or "would like some help" or "should try to find a spiritual director," our society provides an almost overwhelming number of choices, most of which look so much alike on the surface that it may be difficult to distinguish one from another. Moreover, the person himself is not usually completely clear about the real meaning or implications of either the positive or negative life experience that is moving him to seek help. He only knows that talking things over with someone else, getting another point of view, seeing things from a wider perspective or simply "getting things out in the open" in dialogue with another person would be preferable to the isolation and perplexity he is presently experiencing.

These days, in view of the current fascination for natural spiritual experiences and the multiple phenomena of the spiritual revolution presently available in our culture, it is increasingly difficult for men and women impelled by a positive desire to embark on the inward journey, to find what for them will be the best, most fruitful "way" or path. There are many laws of the spiritual journey that can be discovered and mapped out more or less independently of strictly religious considerations; there are likewise many methods leading to meditative self-awareness and inner wakefulness that are capable of bringing people to transcendental consciousness or "centeredness" in their daily lives without leading them any further in the direction of religious faith. We find many well intentioned Christians moving towards Zen Buddhist, Taoist or other Eastern paths in order to attain a sense of unification and ecstasy that their previous faith experience seems to lack. Not recognizing the mystical and "instrumental" possibilities in their own tradition,[1] and feeling a need to link their action in the world with more contemplative modes of being, they may embark on the path of an Eastern tradition that, while it maintains a belief in the spiritual world and keeps alive practices for relating to that world, may very well not be the path that corresponds to the deepest rootedness of their being.

The culture also offers a "smorgasbord" of affectively-oriented techniques of change that are immensely appealing to people whose life experience has been mainly negative, especially in regard to emotional satisfaction. For many such persons, a moment of ego-desperation, of questioning their "reasonable" Western pattern of life, does not lead to the quest for spiritual or even intellectual growth, but results only in an increase of their direct sensate experience of life. The human potential movement with its encounter groups, sensitivity sessions, self-actualizing gestalt and primal-scream therapies seems to speak directly to the alienated, out of touch condition of many men and women in twentieth century Europe and North America. Especially among the middle class, both Christian and non-Christian, people who are neither psychotic or even severely neurotic, are flocking to psychoanalysts, counselors and therapists in search of healing for "the whole person," not just for the isolated mind or psyche. Even when a person comes specifically seeking "spiritual direction," a twentieth century guide must realize that this person's expectations are in all probability deeply influenced by current socio-psychological assumptions about

what it means to be a "whole" person. He or she will have
to be aware that spiritual liberation for these people can
and must include human liberation in terms that will not
deny this wholeness.[2] The spiritual guide must also recognize that unconcealing the Mystery for most contemporary Christians is inextricably bound up with a style of
Christianity that places the struggle for justice, peace and
freedom for all people and not just for certain individuals,
at the center of its concern.

Even prior to deciding to seek out a guide, then, there
are certain expectations, either conscious or unconscious
in the person looking for guidance. These expectations
arise from his own past experiences and encounters, as
well as from his personal hopes or fears about the future,
to say nothing of the social and cultural world in which his
individual life is situated.[3] Unable to articulate fully either
his problem or the world of meaning that is its context, the
person presents himself to a counselor, a teacher, a therapist, a guru, a trusted friend or someone considered experienced in ways of the spirit. He is hoping for help, desiring
to grow, looking for new life. It is the responsibility of the
counselor or spiritual guide to be aware from the beginning of the possible nature of these expectations and to try
to clarify them not only for the sake of the other, but for
the sake of their mutual project. From my own experience,
I know that it is not always possible or even desirable to
begin immediately probing into the other's motives for
coming, into his "hidden agenda" of expectations and resistances. Usually the most I can do is to straighten out in
my own mind what I am ready to offer and to try to help
the other by means of gentle questioning, to see whether
this is what he or she is looking for.

It is up to the guide to have sufficiently distinguished
these various roles and to be as clear as possible about

what can or cannot happen in this particular situation.[4] Not only does this practice demonstrate respect for the concrete reality of the person who comes, it also takes into account the limitations of the guide or director. It will be fruitful to look at three broad areas of "helping" that consciously or unconsciously co-constitute the contemporary person's expectations of guidance situations, and to see from their structure why, although they bear a surface resemblance to, they are not to be identified with, what has so far been described as Christian spiritual direction. However, because each one of these areas is complex in itself, each will suffer from what is necessarily a superficial treatment. There is no intent on my part either to praise or criticize any of these three, but simply to notice how they differ in certain structural points from one another and from the central topic of interest in this book.

The psychotherapy or counseling situation

In our culture, everyone is familiar with this contractual coming together of persons for a certain duration of shared space (commonly an office) and time (usually about an hour) during which one of them specifically intends to use certain skills at his or her command for the psychological growth and betterment of the other. According to the way in which the counselor or psychotherapist perceives reality, she will describe the therapeutic intention in terms ranging from understanding, analysis, advice giving, and behavior change with regard to clients in the "normal" psychic range, up to and including analysis and treatment of personality problems and maladjustments rooted in unconscious conflicts or traumatic experiences of clients in the "abnormal" psychic range. Bracketing for a moment the differences opened up by this description, let us look more generally at the underlying structure of this phenomenon called therapy or counseling or therapeutic counseling.

Roughly speaking, a therapy session is built on one of the basic structures of daily life, that of face to face encounter in which two or more people orient themselves towards the unfolding world of their common experience in the here and now. To this common world of visible social and cultural meanings of their being together, each person comes with an invisible complexity of interrelated personal meanings and values that reach back into past encounters and forward into future intentions. It is this complexity of somewhat failed interrelationships with other people; of anxious confrontation with unexpected events; of isolated and confused feelings about the result, that forms a web in which the client is momentarily caught. During the sessions, as this web unfolds in all its intricacy of meaning for the client, the therapist attempts to enter empathically that world of meaning, to share that perspective on experience that the client is living at the present moment in such a way that the client may decide freely to be, to exist, somewhat differently and thus to change his or her unhappy experience of people, events and things. Most therapists will agree that in therapy, attention must be paid not only to the "figure" — to the actual words of the client telling the story as he sees it in all its emotion-laden immediacy — but also to the invisible "ground" or context of the story, which extends to the limits of this particular client's world-relatedness. The therapist is, in other words, present not only to another troubled human being, but also and at the same time, as much as possible to the invisible value horizons of his lived world.

While it is not possible to quote here the individual opinion of psychotherapists regarding the meaning and goal of their encounter with another human being in the counseling situation, I think that most would agree that "psychotherapy addresses itself to the inner difficulties that interfere with an individual's ability to cope with the tasks and stresses inherent in human life."[5] Probably there would also be rather widespread agreement on the necessity for dealing in the therapeutic relationship with the client's "sense of helplessness, the fear and inner conviction of being unable to 'cope' and to change things."[6] From my own experience as a therapist, I know that the client usually expresses the problem in terms of not knowing what to *do,* or wondering how he or she can functionally manage life better.

It seems then that one aspect proper to psychotherapy or counseling situations in general is that the person who comes is almost always moved primarily by a somewhat negative experience. Such a person is usually finding it difficult to inhabit certain areas of life. They are often out of touch or in bad relationship with other people, with themselves, with their bodies and emotions, or with their societal and work environment. They may be experiencing loneliness, isolation, lack of love or inability to work, accompanied by fear, anxiety, anger, or suspicion. The fact that therapists often describe their concern as being directed towards a troubled or "sick patient" with neurotic "symptoms" and behavior reminds us that psychotherapy was born within the "medical model" paradigm, where illness and problem-solving were the common denominators. Even later, more growth-oriented models that concentrate on attaining psychological health rather than on simply curing illness, usually make the emotional distress of the troubled person their point of departure, and diagnosis and interpretation their major method.

Moreover, descriptions of the therapeutic process seem

to stress interpretation and handling of transference and countertransference reactions, terms pointing directly to the centrality of the relationship between therapist and client in a therapeutic encounter. Often this relationship is depicted as a co-constituting of one personality by the other, or even as a battle of wills where the therapist's techniques are combatted by the client's resistance. Even the description of therapy as a situation where two people interact and "try to come to an understanding of one another" points to the possibility of the collision of two differing value systems. Certainly it is true that even in everyday human encounters that are not set up for the purpose of bringing about change, there is always the possibility of friction because no two people ever emerge from identical worlds of meaning. When we add the probability that the ground of a typical psychotherapy session is the divided and complex social scene of contemporary North American urban civilization and that at least one person in the encounter is determined either to cling to that status quo or avoid becoming adjusted to it, one can see why a harmonious flow "between" client and therapist is not always forthcoming. It is not surprising that in spite of the effort to understand one another, the relational mode of therapy seems to be characterized by a somewhat depersonalized atmosphere in which the persons who are subjects of their own chosen worlds of meaning find it difficult to encounter each other in freedom. Moreover, because of the depersonalizing modes of relationship common to our culture, therapy based on these modes may move in the direction of making the client into an object of the therapist's analysis or cure, thus depriving him even further of his personhood and his relational ability.

Finally, in assessing Bruch's point that therapy has "the specific goal of accomplishing something beneficial for the complaining person,'"[7] I find myself wondering about the direction and depth of that "something." I wonder who decides where on the continuum from mere adaptation to radical transformation of consciousness and spiritual breakthrough each particular client and counselor wants to aim? In cases of psychotic separation from reality, the goal is clear — return to participation of the client with others in a shared world of meaning. The same is true for persons whose life of functioning and relating is somehow paralyzed by obviously compulsive or hysterical obsessions, whose inability to move past blind repetition of infantile modes is seriously interfering with their everyday life. But what about the person who comes to therapy in a state of anxiety, fully in touch with the reality of his world, not obviously impaired or inhibited, but simply finding that very reality itself problematic? Perhaps the person who comes is suffering from the anguish of guilt, or is haunted by "shoulds" for reasons that carry little value in the more pragmatically oriented world of the therapist.[8] Present here can be a subtle contradiction of values which may be entirely unnoticed by either client or therapist, both of whom lack recognition of the fact that underlying obvious problems in functioning and development may be highly variegated worlds of implicit valuing that embody a spiritual directedness of change for each person. This last factor may account for the increasing trend in therapy towards a recognition of the spiritual dimension of life.

Movements towards religious counseling

People seek help not only because they are having problems with specific functional aspects of daily life. As we have already mentioned, moments of ego desperation or loss may open them to previously unnoticed realms of meaning. By the same token the very absence of problems or surfeit of immediate satisfaction may lead some persons to suspect that this is not "all there is."[9] Through the centuries in all cultures and civilizations there has been a greater or lesser recognition of a certain invisible Ground that lies concealed in the immediacy of our taken-for-granted lived experience. Attempts have been made by all manner of guides, religious instructors and directors, spiritual friends and gurus to help people who come to them to awaken to the meaning of the beyond that they have begun to discover in the midst of their encounters with the persons, things and events of daily life.[10] Often this religious helping has taken the form of temporarily withdrawing the person from his usual involvement in daily routines so that he may undertake a meditative journey inwards towards the center of himself and concentrate on states of inner wakefulness and attention for the sake of attaining a transformed consciousness.

Returning for a moment to our previous description of the therapeutic counseling situation, we can make some comparisons that distinguish it from religious counseling. In therapy it is usually taken for granted that both the person seeking help and the helper are not only products of the larger ongoing society, but also that they remain within that horizon of understood meanings during the course of their encounter. Often the aim of the therapeutic relationship is simply to change or adjust the outlook and behavior of the person who comes so that he may more fruitfully inhabit certain partial areas of that culture, such as his marital relationship, his work responsibility, his social, sexual or aesthetic involvements, and so on. In the meeting between a person whose life experiences are pointing him beyond the known to the unknown and a religious guide or guru more familiar with this unknown territory, we find, at least in some traditions, that the guru emphasizes temporarily abandoning the horizon of shared societal objects and meanings for the sake of penetrating beyond them to a realm that is regarded as infinitely more important and lasting. This breakthrough is achieved for the most part via various techniques of meditation, sensory deprivation, fasting, chanting and isolation from certain distracting people, events and things.

Another point that clearly distinguishes what we might call counseling in the religious dimension from therapy as an art of secular society, is that the person who comes seeking the former is not necessarily experiencing his world in a negative way. In fact it is usually only persons who have already attained a certain level of mental, emotional and functional stability who can be open to the dimension of the "more than." Certainly persons when they embark on a religious search may be suffering from neurosis brought on by a lack of spiritual meaning in their life, but the operative paradigm is more likely to lean towards health rather than sickness in such an encounter. It is not surprising that in most traditional forms of guidance centered on the religious dimension, there is not as much attention paid to the "world" of the one who comes. The web of relationships with people, events and things that the person already is, now encounters the world of values and relatedness inhabited by the guru or spiritual director. Without a doubt all the possibilities for collision as well as harmony are present in the encounter. However, what is important is the overarching religious dimension, that is, the ground or depth of their encounter rather than the relationship itself. Even self-exploration seems to be done more for the sake of becoming sensitive to the larger horizon that extends beyond the ego limits of both of them, rather than for the sake of being understood by the other. The focus is on this here and now world only in so far as the directee may learn to discern the "more than" within it.

There is another sense, however, in which the relationship between disciple and guru can be said to carry more weight than it does in the therapy situation. A therapist, even when his reality is concealed by a positive transference,[11] is still recognized by all but the most dependent clients as a limited bearer of values, a less than perfect fellow human with whom one can at times disagree. The traditional guru, however, is immune from such fallibility. He is expected to "be there" already in terms of the world of spiritual meaning into which the person who comes wants to be introduced, to have all the answers, and to be fully experienced in living within that unfamiliar horizon. The relationship between disciple and guru is characterized by an aura of power and prestige, by the implication of knowledge and obligation that goes far beyond that born by the therapist-client relationship.

As for the change, the inner wakefulness, the transformation of consciousness that is to be brought about in and through this relationship, in the general type of encounter we have been describing, much depends on the guru's or the teacher's presence, but there is also much that the disciple can do by way of self-discipline. He can avoid distraction and abstain from the sense pleasures of this world as well as employ specific techniques of breathing, chanting, dancing and concentration to aid the process of transformation of self. In most cases the goal itself seems to be clear. The master can recognize when the disciple has finally attained it. The disciple in these religious traditions, having changed from a state of sleep to a state of wakefulness, is likened to one who has reached "nirvana," attained the "Buddha nature," is in "white light," or, in the Zen tradition, has passed beyond the diminished modes of consciousness where the subject-object dichotomy prevails, and has reached an awareness of "Pure Being."

The pastoral counseling movement

In the Western Christian tradition we find people through the centuries recognizing the depth dimension that underlies their everyday experience and looking to the official churches, religious leaders and other helping people to point out the way of participating in this value, especially when they must make ethical or moral decisions in relation to their life situations.[12] Although directly involved with the life of faith, the pastoral counseling movement compares closely with the therapeutic counseling model already described. In fact one of the major concepts of the movement, the "cure of souls," seems particularly appropriate in that pastoral counseling originated in the clinical training of hospital chaplains who were among the first to combine psychotherapeutic theory with pastoral practice. Recognizing some sort of connection between troubled emotional states and spiritual crises; between personal, sexual development and mature religion; between daily decisions and deeper spiritual motivation; between family and social difficulties and lack of spiritual resources; between caring for bodily and interpersonal needs and caring for the soul, contemporary clergy, teachers, religious consultants and now doctors, nurses and social workers have developed forms of counseling that borrow heavily from psychiatric as well as theological resources.[13]

Relying on the medical model, pastoral counseling

seems to be concerned primarily with troubled people whose problems and negative experiences are similar to those that send clients to therapists. Their afflictions are usually described in clinical terms and many of the techniques employed in psychotherapeutic situations are used to help, heal, guide, sustain and reconcile the client who comes for consultation. The pastoral counselor sees his role extending beyond clinical terms, however; often he assumes that his intervention in the life of this person will be received by him as emerging from the counselor's Christian concern. For the most part, such pastoral counselors are dedicated persons of much good will, whose own personal lives are lived in openness to the Sacred or to a system of Christian values that could give both breadth and depth to their dealing with other people. They are usually trained in theology and come from a religiously oriented background. However, their formal clinical training is sometimes not very profound and may well consist of a fairly eclectic amalgam of Freudian, Jungian, transactional, gestalt and a variety of other theories. A pastoral counselor's approach will often combine some Rogerian non-directive notions of acceptance and mutual respect with more radical confrontation techniques to deal with aggression and encourage personal responsibility.

Since this type of counseling emerges directly out of the situation the person is finding difficult, these counselors may also be armed with further techniques for dealing with alcoholism, marital problems, juvenile delinquency, homosexuality, suicide, school counseling, religious pathology, ministering to the dying, and so on. They will most likely be in touch with the newer theologies and theological ideas regarding issues like liberation, abortion, racism, sexism, Christian social involvement, charismatic prayer and the latest insights into Western adaptation of

Eastern meditation techniques.

Because this style of counseling is rooted in the Western Christian tradition, we find the counseling relationship itself tending towards a mix of nurturing, consoling, acceptance, and non-judgmental support of the one who comes, with perhaps an emphasis on non-possessive warmth, respect for the other and empathic confrontation. Its Christian roots also appear in its concern for openness to the Spirit and for oppressed persons, exploited classes, despised races and dominated countries. Often the pastoral counselor's values reflect his concern for the struggle for justice, peace and freedom which may or may not be echoed in the clients' more personal exploration of their inner selves. It is not surprising that at times in the midst of all these interesting focuses of attention, either the counselor or the client, or perhaps both, may lose sight of the deeper mysterious "whole" of which all these realities are but partial manifestations.

It may even become difficult to suggest clearly the goal of whatever change is to be brought about. At a certain point, the Christian or pastoral counselor may ask: Is the client to be helped physically, psychically, morally, spiritually? Does the relationship aim merely at adjustment to the status quo, or is there a need for social change as well? Can "peace of mind" be preferred over "peace of soul?" Do the individual needs of the person who comes take precedence over the broader needs of the group to which he or she belongs? Is the aim to transform his behavior or situation, his attitudes or consciousness? Might there be more "sanity" in revolting against a culture that has lost its spiritual transcendence? Can a deep spiritual transformation be brought about in encounters where issues of sin and guilt are ignored or where there is little or no serious attempt to join action to contemplation? These and similar questions may occur also to the ordained minister or priest who, in the course of the sacramental rite of reconciliation, finds occasions where short term situational counseling or some sort of spiritual direction seems indicated.

Clearly, spiritual direction does not necessarily include confessional counseling. Nor does it approach the same variety of difficult situations as does pastoral counseling. Spiritual direction, although it often deals with much of the same life material, is not to be confused with therapeutic counseling either. Although it strongly resembles some aspects of the guidance described in the section on movements towards religious counseling, it also differs from them, especially from those in the Eastern traditions.

This brief glance at three familiar contemporary encounters shows us that they look like but are not identical with spiritual direction. To come to an understanding of the latter, we must go back again to that moment in human experience when a person desiring something "more" seeks out someone to guide him or her in that search.

CHAPTER V

A NATURAL FOUNDATION FOR
SPIRITUAL DIRECTION

Human desire for the Real

Whether we reflect on the crowds that flocked to Jesus and the early Christian guides like John, Paul and Anthony, or whether we shift our gaze to people in the twentieth century seeking guidance and direction from a variety of religious counselors and/or psychotherapists, we cannot help but recognize a connecting link. What seekers seem to want most is to transcend themselves, to live in a larger horizon, to seek what is of real value. They want to partake in some way of the life that is "more than" what they experience ordinarily in their day to day existence. This capacity for natural mysticism[1] seems to be common to people of all times and nations. It manifests itself both in momentary peak-experiences[2] and in a slowly dawning awareness over the years of an all-encompassing whole that is the context of everyday experience. Expressing itself in many different ways as a search for "wholeness," for "self fulfillment," for "ecstasy," this quest in its nonreligious form constitutes a natural foundation for the spiritual life in its fullness as a mystery of grace.[3]

"Awakened" persons engaged in this quest are reluctant to categorize it from the point of view either of religious or of pastoral counseling. Some find the transcendent ground of the former too far removed from the here and now concreteness of daily life; others feel over-absorption of the latter in the immanent aspects of personal and/or social situations tends to obscure access to the "more than." Such persons seek a non-dualistic world view that, instead of separating them from either the spiritual or the temporal world of meaning, will harmonize these worlds and integrate the human person within them. On the one hand, they are reluctant to lose touch with the natural richness of the daily here and now; on the other, they want to avoid absolutizing any one societal or personal value system as this might create a "false immanence" that could be mistaken for the source of transcendent life. Thus, many people today are searching for a type of counseling that trusts both the laws of natural creation and their transcendent context; that is capable of directing both counselor and client, guru and disciple, as well as teachers, students, speakers, audiences, therapists, friends — in fact, all human beings — towards their fullest possibilities by widening and deepening their consciousness of the *context* of that life as it is being lived here and now. Are there links that connect this contemporary non-religious search with the Christian practice of spiritual direction?

First of all let us look at what is happening outside the Church apart from Christian revelation. The contemporary consciousness revolution is not only uncovering the natural foundations of the life of grace; in the process it is revolutionizing both the ground and figure of traditional clinical therapeutic encounters as well. We find "awakened" contemporary clients demanding "more" of the therapeutic situation itself.[4] Although not inclined to accept any specific revealed tradition as the context for their restructuration of consciousness, clients want to move beyond the narrow outlook of cultural immediacy. They want to include in this restructuring of conscious presence, the "more" of Reality that has so far eluded them. They are witnessing to a trend already apparent for several decades in the area of counseling and therapy — towards increased recognition of the transpersonal dimension.[5]

Changing goals of therapy

Awareness of one's personal need for transcendence on the part of both clients and counselors, together with the contemporary tendency to deal with questions of personal identity and ultimate meaning in a psychological rather than a religious context, has led to a certain blurring of the lines that used to divide therapy from spiritual guidance, psychological practice from sacred tradition.[6] At its inception psychology, like other sciences, confined its interest and concentration to several more or less defined aspects of the human personality, for example, the areas of sexual, social, functional, individual and intellectual behavior.[7] Today psychologists are interested in the aspirations of the whole person for meaning and peak-experiences. We find psychological and psychoanalytic literature and conferences beginning to deal with mystic, oceanic, aesthetic and creative experiences, and with love, parental, religious and insight experiences, to name only a few.[8]

It takes a wise and experienced guide to discern the unarticulated horizon that gives these intensely human experiences their meaning for the person who comes for guidance. For example, how does the therapist distinguish the spiritual horizon that gives meaning to a specific religious experience? How much does he or she have to know of the difference between the prerevealed or revealed horizons of this experience? How can they, without special training in theology or philosophy, guide persons whose transpersonal experience involves the articulation of horizons of transcendent meaning that are unfamiliar to them? Not surprisingly the majority, both within and without the psychological disciplines, are simply unable to meet the challenge of this growing demand for guidance in areas beyond their professional competence.

The therapeutic aim of restructuring conscious presence to reality continues to retain a basic hidden directedness towards freedom, towards going beyond immediacy in view of a larger horizon. Whether it is expressed in terms like "coping with and adjustment to stress," "mental health," "emancipation from embeddedness in neurotic object-relations," "liberation from infantile defenses," "self-fulfillment and actualization" or "realization of true self-identity," therapeutic change involves a thrust towards liberation from limitations. These limitations may be embodied in the self, in the confines of the social and cultural milieu, or in one's view of reality in general. The therapist's goal is to allow, by means of reflection on these experiences, a new way of seeing them to emerge. As a new consciousness of self and world comes to the fore, the cognitive context of cherished ideas that framed these problems and disrupted the person's life is restructured; personal strengths are discerned beneath pathology; the client moves towards an increase in personal freedom.

The shift towards meditative presence

In therapeutic practice, a definite connection has emerged between freedom, change and the human capacity for reflection on experience. Therapy is now seen by many as a meditative discipline aimed at an inner awakening of the whole person, as a seeing beyond "what seems to be the case" to what really is.[9] This shift in some current therapies, which involves placing their aims beyond mere symptom removal and adjustment to cultural demands, may be due in some degree to the influence of the Eastern gurus, to Zen and other related diciplines that aim at awakening the human person from his embeddedness in the world of phenomenal appearances and putting him in contact with reality. The overall aim of such disciplines is not that the person will necessarily feel better, but that ignorance will be relieved, the mind, enlightened, and as a consequence authentic being will be attained. Such liberation from unreal valuing and pretentions already transcends the more popular forms of counseling techniques designed simply to help people get along better with others or adjust to the demands of society. Most persons bring to a counseling situation such familiar kinds of anxiety as personal and social worries about status in one's group or family, the fear of disclosure as a phony or misfit, anxiety about not being liked or of losing one's cherished securities and achievements. These anxieties are exposed as almost irrelevant in a horizon that transcends a merely natural way of thinking.[10] In these more "whole" therapeutic situations, the client is encouraged to move beyond the taken-for-granted pragmatism of the world of ego-level concerns. He is helped to perceive both self and others in a wider horizon that stretches beyond the mundane achievement of practical goals and purposes; to choose freely certain absolute values as his own.[11]

Clearly, the increased desire for "wholeness" in the culture has played a part in this shift from isolated self searching to a more dialogic presence to the meaning of problems in relation to a whole of which they are merely parts. After a long period of alienation and individualism, people today are once more seeking to recover their rootedness, their sense of belonging in a reality greater than themselves. Fewer and fewer thinking people are willing to deal with vital and psychological problematics concerning partial aspects of created reality like sex, politics, economics, functioning, the arts, or even religion, in isolation from a wider context of meaning that connects all of these parts and in which they can feel rooted and at home themselves. The implications of this emphasis on wholeness are gradually finding expression in the way therapists and counselors approach the goal of change. Attention continues to be paid to what happens intrapsychically to the individual in terms of alleviating his personal suffering, guilt, pain, anxiety and negative interpersonal experiences. However, therapists and counselors are also increasingly aware of other "finite provinces of meaning"[12] with which one's wider consciousness is potentially in relation.

It is not surprising then to find psychiatrists, counselors and teachers, exploring and incorporating into their practice many of the meditative methods and techniques used in the great religious traditions to alter the nature of conscious awareness. As efforts to liberate people from selective, rubricized modes of perception incorporate more and more not only of the techniques and vocabulary of the Sufi, Tibetan, Buddhist and Zen disciplines but also the context to which these techniques belong, some Western psychotherapists are beginning to sound like religious teachers. Moreover, getting oneself "together" via yoga, TM or gestalt techniques and/or by means of following one of the many spiritual "paths" has become, for much of the population, a way of attaining what I see as the therapeutic goal of widening and deepening consciousness of the context of one's behavior.[13] The rediscovery by the West of Eastern disciplines, with their physical and psychological exercises and techniques of meditation, coincides with a recognition that psychoanalytic and other psychological movements of our time do not in themselves achieve the clarity of thinking and quality of consciousness attainable by these traditional methods. It would be well for persons called to be Christian spiritual directors to realize that equally effective practical psychological methods and instrumental forms were originally part of our heritage also.[14]

Reflective living and therapy

Meditative self-presence is a technique familiar to all who are interested in the spiritual life. The basis for contemplative living in former ages, it is now being incorporated into contemporary therapeutic practice. The reflective ability to bend back on concrete situated aspects of one's experience, to question the invisible meaning of one's encounters with reality in its oppressiveness, false values, misery, loneliness and death as well as in its happier manifestations, is a sign of human freedom. Without the ability to slow down the vital-reactive life of impulse and defensiveness, to stop and think, to reflect before reacting to a stimulus, people would be caught in the closed circuit of the S-R paradigm.[15] Without the ability to take a reflective distance from the immediacy of daily encounters with reality, people remain locked in habitual fixations and illusions about themselves and their own relational life. Without the ability to stand back from the everyday round, we would soon lose the capacity even to imagine a larger whole of which our small concerns are only a part. Connections between seemingly separate parts of reality are lost; choices become less frequent and automatic reactions may take over.

A totally unreflective human being would lose touch

with himself, with others, and with the meaningfulness of his world. The liberating effects of change that are the aim of the therapeutic encounter would not be experienced; whatever paralyzing one-sidedness led the person to seek help in the first place could not be brought into perspective. Immersed in an ego-functional society with its alienating orientation towards having rather than being, we contemporary North Americans would, in fact often do, experience a repression of both vitality and spirituality in exchange for the illusion of prediction and control that our rigid encapsulation seems to provide.

Reflective or meditative living can break up closed reactive circuits; it can wake people out of sleepy routine perspectives, help tune out alienating distractions, and center awareness on hidden spiritual meaning. This possibility, inherent in every person, explains why both so many contemporary psychologists and some spiritual directors propose to restructure conscious presence to reality by means of reflection on experience. Both suggest, for example, that their clients or directees keep journals. In one sense, the therapy situation is, for the client, comparable to keeping a journal of the week's events. He must slow down sufficiently to look again at what has actually happened; to try and make sense out of the persons, events and things of his everyday life against the horizon of that life; to recognize the ways in which he must change cherished behavior patterns that are constricting his life and causing pain to self and others. For many people, this encounter with a therapist is the first time they have consistently reflected on the meaning of their life. In asking why, since it accomplishes so much that is valuable, so many avoid serious reflection on experience unless forced to do so by circumstances beyond their control, we fail to understand how little the human person actually desires to be made aware of his reactive and defensive patterns, or how anxiously he clings to all the familiar obstacles that stand in the way of changing them. Letting go of fixed positions that have come to mean security for the individual implies giving up control; it calls for a creative "destruction" of the carefully constructed illusions of one's life. It means leaving oneself open to the unpredictable in life. For many such a surrender is too difficult to sustain.

This same capacity for reflection in distancing people from reality in its immediacy, could also encapsulate them further in a fantasy world of their own making unless there is from time to time some guidance to keep them from making this an isolated within-the-skin process of reflecting on ideology rather than on real life. Without a therapist or guiding other, the reflective process can also divorce persons from their relation to the wider reality that comprises their intersubjective shared world; it can encase them further in illusions resulting from introspection. It is precisely introspective narrowness and the resultant fear of relating beyond the limits of ego control that keep people from opening themselves to broader and deeper horizons. Not only therapists, but spiritual directors also are discovering that without some destruction of the illusion of control, without a minimum of surrender and leaving the self open to the unpredictable, neither client nor directee can become truly free for union with the mysterious ground of all that is. In encouraging their clients to shift towards a more meditative, less controlling stance in the face of reality, it would seem that many contemporary therapists are rediscovering one of the natural foundations for the graced life of faith.

Faith as the context of spiritual direction

An increasing number of priests, religious counselors and spiritual directors are paying attention to the light shed on their endeavor by the psychologist's insight into the value of reflective living and meditative practice. As they come to a greater understanding of Divine Mystery, they are forced to acknowledge that it not only resists penetration by psychological techniques of measurement, diagnostic labelling and control by manipulation; it also does not yield even to the more "spiritual" techniques of various popular meditative methods and approaches.[16] From an empirical point of view, there is in fact little difference between bio-feedback results for a TM meditator repeating a mantra and a Christian monk immersed in the "Jesus prayer."[17] Both reach the state of alpha or even theta; in both the biological rhythms are slowed down, and both can be measured in terms of their attainment of transformed consciousness.

However, in spite of the fact that both can be compared scientifically, there are aspects of the Christian experience of mystery that cannot be reduced to quantifiable terms. There is, for instance, no valid extrapolation or a merely psychological explanation of meditative reflection that would allow us to apply it to the mystery of the monk's growth in love for God through opening himself to penetration by grace. This latter perspective belongs to the life of faith, to the invisible, impenetrable realm of graced reality of which Jesus Christ is God's ultimate revelation. Once again we find ourselves confronting the question of the exact nature of Christian spiritual direction. It is not psychotherapy or counseling; nor is it easily identified with ordinary religious or even pastoral counseling; yet it seems to have a natural affinity for these disciplines. Has anyone ever set out the parameters of Christian spiritual direction in its proper context, which is faith in the revelation of Christ, the Son of God?

In his letter to the Ephesians, St. Paul has done just that — beginning with the broadest possible horizon of the mystery of salvation and of the Church.[18] In Chapter 1, he describes the "more than," the sacred horizon in which we are already rooted, as the Mystery of the Father's will, which the Father manifested from all eternity in Christ. Thus, he names the numinous transcendent context that is the loving ground not only of all human encounters, but of the larger universes of meaning in which they take place. In words that rejoice in the goodness of creation and in all levels of the created self, he points to the presence of a new creation in God's plan of salvation that is meant to incorporate all of the human self's daily experience in a "pneumatized" life of grace. Within this gifted horizon of God's love, all people and the universe itself are to be redeemed from their alienated condition; they are to be brought back from their dividedness, from their out of touchness with themselves, with each other and with God, who is the source of all truth and life.[19] Paul speaks directly to alienated, sinful, defensive human estrangement from intimacy with God. He speaks to closed hearts shut off from life in a one-dimensional pursuit of immanence, in the worship of false gods. In Chapter 5, he calls upon people to wake up from their sleep and to try to discover what the Lord wants of them, to discern the direction that the Father has planned for each unique human being from before the beginning of time.[20]

In Chapter 4, he indicates the type of change that must take place: a radical transformation and restructuration of the whole vital and psychic self, a "spiritual revolution"[21] in which the old idolatrous self with its illusions is put aside so that the new self may shine forth in the world. A similar giving up of an old way of life, a conversion or renewal of heart and mind, seems to be essential for spiritual growth in all great religious traditions. The transformation itself may be expressed in different terminology, but the aim is the same. Paul's prayer that the Father enlighten the eyes of their minds (or hearts) so that they can perceive in a new way the invisible presence of Christ working among them[22] reminds us again that the initiative for this new view of reality is ultimately not to be found in the effort and good will of either apostle or convert, teacher or learner, counselor or client, guru or disciple, but is actually a gift of the Father's merciful love that brings people back to life in Christ at the very moment when they are dead to this life through sin.[23]

What then, in Paul's view, is the role of the spiritual director if it is not to accomplish all this by skillful techniques and insight? How is he or she to draw the person out of alienation and into the house where God lives in the Spirit? In describing himself in Chapter 3 as "servant of the Mystery,"[24] and explainer of how it is to be dispensed, Paul gives an excellent insight into what a spiritual director should see as his primary task. Putting his confidence in the Father's love, Paul, as director, asks only that the hidden unique identity of each one in his care will be discovered and grow strong, so that Christ may be their director, so that He may live in their hearts through faith, and that, planted and built on love, each one may have the strength to grasp the breadth and length and height and depth until knowing the love of Christ (which yields not to knowledge but only to mystical awareness of being loved), they may be filled with the utter fullness of God.[25]

For Paul, this mysterious transformation comes about

precisely within the everyday life situation of each human person no matter what the external circumstances of that situation may be. That is to say, he sees each person as a whole self, a vital-personal embodied spirit, a unity that emerges via its participation in the real here and now world of situated concrete other persons, daily events and given things.[26] As we see in Chapter 6, for Paul, a person's spiritual life is not divided off from his or her daily experience of incarnation and participation, of interpersonal relations, of manual work and leisure, of sexuality and prayer, of the unique contribution each is able to make to the building of the Christian community, the body of Christ; nor is it separated from all the difficulties, disappointments, losses and heartaches that this existence inevitably involves. In Paul's world view, no aspect of the person's past, present or future is excluded from the lived relation with mystery that his or her life is meant to be. At the core then of the encounter between Paul and a believing Ephesian, is an awareness of depth and meaning that transcends both, a primitive awareness of the Mystery that emerges from their (and our) daily experiences of loneliness, fear and death, or solidarity, security and faith, and that is the basis of their interest in what their "spiritual director" has still to reveal to them of its meaning.

Like people of our time, the Ephesians seek direction and guidance in the life of the Spirit out of a positive desire for the "more than" that lies behind the vital-functional ordinariness of their everyday experience and that of their society and culture. A glimpse of its illusory quality, a moment of reflective distance from its immediacy, an awareness of the contingency of all that appears has led them to look beyond the visible to the invisible. They seek the transcendent in and through the immanent, while avoiding both the absolutization and the exclusion of either. The "bare bones" of the spiritual guidance situation set forth in the Epistle to the Ephesians involves the coming together of the people of Ephesus and Paul; the ensuing collision of different worlds of meaning; and a reflective exchange in which their director, the servant of the Mystery, discloses values emerging from a realm of meaning relatively unknown to them. At each step along the way they are free to decide whether to reject or put into practice these spiritual values that inevitably put them at odds with their own society and culture and sometimes even with members of their family and circle of friends.

Jesus himself was the model for Paul and all other spiritual directors of this kind when he came telling people to repent, change, convert their lives because a new creation — a new world of meaning and values — the Kingdom of God, was at hand. He spent the rest of his life helping people to abandon their false preconceptions about this Kingdom of God. Gradually he unfolded the meaning of this mystery for them and slowly transformed their realization of the reign of God that was already among them, underlying their everyday life. Like Paul, he referred all the glory of this new creation to his Father and the Spirit of Christ whose power working in us can do infinitely more than we can ask or imagine.[27] It is within this context of the Mystery of the Holy Spirit working within the person that it will be possible to identify more precisely the aims and purposes of specifically Christian spiritual direction.

CHAPTER VI

SPIRITUAL DIRECTION OF CHRISTIANS

The source of spiritual direction

As spiritual director, Jesus was primarily interested in unconcealing the hidden mystery of His Father's loving initiative towards human beings. In dialogue with individuals or groups, he wanted to bring about that deep change, or metanoia, that would affect their subsequent perception of every aspect of their life. The early Christian understanding of the baptismal event had similar repercussions in the direction of new seeing on the part of those who received it. Then, too, the pattern of unconcealment and fresh perception after metanoia persisted among the earliest of the "Abbas" or spiritual fathers. For all of them, the heart of spiritual direction was to be found in the openness of the director and the people who came for direction to the initiative of God the Father, Son and Holy Spirit, as it permeated the whole of their personality. It was the Holy Spirit, not the human director who was the source of spiritual formation. Among the people of God, there was little chance that the primary role of the spiritual director would be seen as one of educating or moulding persons, or even as solving their problems. For them, the spiritual director was there to allow the aspiring human spirit to act freely, to facilitate the person's contact and cooperation with the Holy Spirit. He then "decreased"[1] as the person grew and as his relationship with God "increased" in contemplative prayer and repentance for sin. Through the ages the Church has never lost sight of this realization that persons cannot enter into an intimate relationship with God, cannot grow in the spiritual life, unless they are led there by the inspiration of the Holy Spirit.[2]

In the twentieth century spiritual direction still aims at the gradual permeation of our being by the divine life implanted at Baptism. As we have seen, there exists a multitude of complexities and questions that nuance the participation of both the person in our secular society who seeks spiritual guidance and the one who feels called upon to respond to that search in the spiritual direction encounter. Current definitions of spiritual direction,[3] each one more or less adequate, can never fully encompass this complexity; they can never define ahead of time what the Spirit will initiate in any concrete situation. Like the people who sought out Jesus, contemporary men and women come from an infinite variety of positive and negative circumstances. Some are seeking mainly integration and depth as they advance and grow in their relationship to the Trinity; others simply need immediate help with a faith crisis or other type of loss of direction such as sin or temptation to sin.

Moreover, contemporary people may be struggling on several levels at once with obstacles to this relationship. What a person states that he or she is looking for spiritual direction and then brings forward not only obstacles to faith but also, and inevitably, problems in the area of emotional growth, interpersonal life and social adjustment, it takes a clear-headed director to be able either to deal with all of these as they directly affect the person's relationship to God and his or her life in Christ, or to refer the person to a therapist, pastoral counselor, confessor or other competent guide. Often the person who comes has only a vague idea of what to expect from spiritual direction. It is the responsibility of the director to be aware of the nuances that differentiate spiritual direction from its psychological, pastoral, and ethical look-alikes and not add to the person's already anxious and tense state by confusing areas or attempting to handle questions for which he or she has little or no competence.

Returning for a moment to Paul's letter to the people of Ephesus, we see that he confronts what we might call psychological problems of estrangement or out-of-touchness with the Divine due to the narrowness and fear of "shut up" hearts embedded in egoistic ways of being, doing and seeing; he points to the need for breaking out of this defensive, controlled, isolating life style by means of a restructuration of conscious perception; but while doing so, he never loses sight of the ultimate destiny of their "spiritual revolution" — union with God in Christ through the Spirit. This highest transformation involves a disclosure to them of the objective Mystery that will henceforth be the revealed ground or horizon of their daily perception of reality. It also attempts to help each of them to recognize how to participate in that Mystery by subjectively absorbing and living out those aspects most appropriate for the person as a unique, concrete, individual with all the personality problems and sinful tendencies such consciousness entails. Paul saw in-depth faith in God's love for the world as the transforming power that would change the baptized person's intentional relation to all persons, events and things. The whole of reality could then be perceived anew as emerging from this love and as worthy of having love bestowed upon it according to the will of the Lord.

In his Epistles he directs people towards the realization that the sinful inclinations, neurotic tendencies and psychological and societal "hang-ups" they bring to any situation cannot preclude the new life of grace that is the "already there" structure of all daily attempts to enter into the struggle at the heart of the universe between light and darkness, love and egoism, trust and fear, peace and war, life and death. This "spiritual warfare" exists not only in each human heart, but also in each human community and country; it goes on between the communities and countries of this world. The transforming vision of reality underlying the aim of Paul's spiritual direction is that of the present and future Kingdom announced by Jesus to which each person is destined by the very fact of his having been born.

An example of transformed perception

One of the traditional ways in which scripture speaks of the new way of seeing reality that accompanies conversion of heart, is to compare it to the transition from blindness to sight.[4] Paul's experience of conversion demonstrates this shift, for he himself moved from thinking he saw reality as it was and acting accordingly, through a period of blindness in which he saw and could do nothing, to a new vision of reality that disclosed the meaning of his acts in an entirely new horizon and changed their direction.[5] The people he had been persecuting in the name of God became, in the light of his faith in the resurrection, the members of Christ's body. This "new seeing" radically altered his experience of those people and, as a consequence, transformed his concrete actions towards them.

As his world view changed, his way of attending to reality underwent a shift from perceiving only its separated parts to an intuition of its meaning as a whole. That whole, as he now saw in a moment of enlightenment by the Holy Spirit, was the Father's plan of unity and peace as revealed by Christ. In his conversion experience, Paul was liberated from his blindness. The scales fell from his eyes;

he no longer saw merely fragmented parts of reality, but a connected whole. He saw the invisible meaning behind the persons, events and things of the visible world. He was liberated from the partial meanings, from the idolatrous, self-serving narrowness of spirit that had concealed this divine meaning from him. He was freed by his new vision to go beyond the old self and become a new person in Christ. The resulting thrust towards transcendence took the form of longing to be with Christ in the Kingdom on the one hand, and, on the other, of spending the rest of his life in loving service for the members of that Kingdom here on earth. Exteriorly he became reabsorbed in trying to achieve a multitude of practical goals and purposes, but interiorly he now saw all the parts of life as figural against a divine ground that was the living person of Jesus Christ.

This spiritual transition from blindness to seeing that views things in the light of spiritual meanings is obviously not the result of "techniques" of consciousness transformation. The initiative that stopped Paul in his tracks, that knocked him to the ground and blinded him, came from beyond his own power. The jolting nature of this event not only broke the circle of his taken-for-granted embeddedness in complacent assumptions, but also forced him to retire from his activities for three years in order to take a reflective look at his experience. Paul was not merely the passive recipient of this marginal event. By cooperating with it, by accepting his own vulnerability, and by not putting up a series of fresh defenses against this unexpected new awareness, he allowed himself to be awakened and brought into a wider field of consciousness.[6] Changed interiorly by this event, he disposed himself more and more for grace.

St. Paul underwent a transformation of the natural consciousness that belonged to his isolated rational intellect as well as of the supraconscious power of presence that belonged to his potentiality for spiritual presence. He became aware of his relation to the "already there" Mystery as a personal presence. This awareness was a pure gift of the Divine Giver, a gift that no technique or instrumental form of the great religious traditions could possibly bring about of themselves.[7] Spiritual direction has, of course, to take into account the normal evolution of consciousness throughout the spiritual development process; at times, it draws upon the help of psychological and psychiatric skills to recognize and analyze various rational and irrational states of consciousness. However, spiritual direction as such aims beyond purely immanent states of consciousness towards the living personal Presence who transcends all creation, and who is the divine object not only of the creature's rational consciousness, but of the desire that pervades his or her whole being as well.

In light of its goal of union with the living Trinitarian God, the transformation which is the goal of spiritual direction involves not merely the person's consciousness or intellect, but the totality of his or her life, as symbolized by the "heart."[8] This kind of direction fosters a change that touches all levels of human life and penetrates to the core of the person's being where he or she meets God, decides in the direction of "yes" or "no," accepts Christ in faith, and is open to His love. Jesus himself spoke not only to the rational intellect of people, but to their hearts in stories and parables based on their everyday life experience. It was through their reflection on these experiences that some of them came to feel at home in the new horizon from which the Kingdom was emerging and found their own direction in bearing fruit for its sake. In speaking to their hearts, Jesus called people to a new life of faith, hope and love, a life that still remains the goal of Christian spiritual direction.

The part played by experience

From what we read in the Acts of the Apostles and in the Epistles, the lives of the first Christians seem to have been permeated by concrete experiences of the victory of Christ and of the reality of the indwelling of God. The Spirit of God, by means of contemplative knowledge or wisdom, provided them with an experiential recognition of the deep mysteries available only to the "spiritual man."[9] Imbued with this lived understanding of the "more than," their daily actions also underwent a transformation. People remarked on the quality of their life. Members of the community of believers were called followers of the "Way." Contemporary Christians do not seem to be as familiar or as in touch with a similar mystical awareness of the spiritual dimensions of everyday reality. For the most part they disclaim any awareness of specifically religious experience. They look with either suspicion or awe upon saints, mystics or other friends of God who speak of having experienced the Invisible Reality that underlies the daily appearances of their world. They also point out, and quite correctly, that some persons simply are more sensitive to the whole experiential realm, a factor that might account for their own seeming lack in this area. However, even the experientially insensitive generation that inhabits twentieth century North American secular society is beginning, with or without faith in a revealed Trinitarian God, to pay more attention to the glimpses of Invisible Reality they discover in the people, events and things of their daily experience. We can expect then, that some of the men and women who seek spiritual direction in this generation do so because they have "had an experience" that has made them stop and think. Certainly they may not have undergone an extraordinary experience of light and vision as Paul did. Granted, some seek direction because they have figuratively been jolted out of their natural attitude by an experience of "ego-desperation," of serious loss, or of personal confrontation with illness or death. But the majority of contemporary seekers come out of much less dramatic circumstances. Like the apostles, the scope of their daily experience is fairly mundane. They are involved in ordinary jobs and professions with opportunities for good and evil. They are made happy and sad. They talk and listen, do dishes, care for their children, work with other people, take buses, pay taxes, read poems, drive cars, do the shopping, go for a walk, fall in love, watch life change around them — in short, they experience life unfolding in relation to the people, events and things of their world to which they are immediately present. These concrete realities appear in their lives and are encountered on several levels; they evoke vital feelings, functional organization, aesthetic appreciation, or all three at the same time. Such is the "stuff of life," the data of our daily experience.

It is possible to live life exclusively on these levels, but for most human beings, either in childhood or thereafter, there comes a moment when it is not the person, event or thing that is figural, but its mysterious ground. A mother feels a moment of ecstasy as she catches sight of the perfection of her baby's fingernail; a worried young man is lifted out od his world of personal insecurity and doubt as he listens to a symphony; a child glimpses something of how great God must be from glorying in the strength and power of his dad.[10] Analysis of the "bare bones" structure of each of these fairly ordinary experiences discloses a human person (mother, young man, child) immediately present in a sensing, pragmatic and attentive manner (bathing, listening, admiring) to a concrete figure (baby, symphony, father) in the ordinary everyday world (of child care, music, having a father). Suddenly, and almost imperceptibly, there is a shift in focus. The person becomes present to the "more than" that transcends the originally experienced person, event or thing. Perception now discloses an all-encompassing world of meaning, the invisible ground of what is seen, heard and touched. The spiritual capacity in the mother, the young man, the child has been awakened; each has become aware of and fascinated by an all-emcompassing horizon they themselves cannot encompass, manage or control, but which itself encompasses and controls all that is. This capacity to be attracted and fascinated, awed or frightened by the Mystery of All That Is, this ability for encounter with the numinous side of reality, is a natural capacity for life on the level of the Spirit, common to all people who have ever lived. Throughout the ages men and women have attempted to cope with these spiritual experiences of fascination and awe. Benign experiences of wonder before the Great Beyond have in many traditions led to paths of contemplative presence to the sacred horizon. Harsh or negative experiences of this uncontrollable, unpredictable "otherness" have resulted in magic and superstitious religious practices, as humans attempt to cope with their fear and anxiety in the face of All That Is.

It has been suggested that even though ours is perhaps the most pragmatic civilization that ever existed, it is finally awakening from embeddedness in its "technological trance" and recognizing the numinous sacred order breaking out at a thousand different points of our experience.[11] Men and women are becoming aware of their innate capacity for new modes of presence to their immediate experience and its sacred horizon as well. Their growing sense of being carried by an infinitely mysterious ground can be, and often is, triggered by natural experiences that have no direct relation to any particular revelation of God, or even to religion as such. However, such experiences do seem to be conditioned by a certain stilling of the other modes of being, a centering into a more contemplative style of presence, an ability to dwell with a phenomenon long enough so that its depth dimensions may disclose itself. This centered awareness of the whole can also be repressed by focusing too immediately on one or the other of the parts. In the examples above, what if the mother had only been able to concern herself with her task of getting the baby clean? What if the young man had not taken time out to listen to the music? What if the child had fearfully to avoid his father's anger?

As mentioned previously, some people are naturally more gifted in sensibility for spiritual experiences than others; similarly some cultures foster this capacity more than others. Fortunately, all cultures have at least a few seers and hearers whose experiential breakthroughs to greater unity have provided the rest of us with landmarks and even complete maps of this territory which, to them, becomes as familiar as home.[12] They are the ones who help us break down ego-functional barriers so that the "already there" spiritual reality may rush in.

Like a sea, spiritual reality surrounds us on all sides. As a Taoist legend reminds us, we keep looking in different places for the water instead of stilling ourselves and discovering that, like fishes, we are "already in" the sea. We are already surrounded by the "more than" to which we belong and where we are ultimately at home. A rejection of alienation and homelessness, a search for rootedness in the whole, has always been part of the story of the human race. We long to be at-home in our destiny; we search for nirvana, for ecstasy, for eternal life, for the heavenly city, for the lost Paradise, for the Grail, for the unifying ground of all that is. This restless quest to understand the "secret," to attain our heart's desire, has been the underlying motivation of saints and holy people throughout time. The universal ability for spiritual presence to the horizon of concrete experiences, for "natural mysticism," is in all human beings the contact point for revelation. It is the core of our being as embodied spirit. It is a point at which the Holy Spirit seems, in our time, to be making his presence felt. This basic possibility, when actuated, often brings people to the point of seeking out some sort of spiritual guidance or direction. Experience of this horizon may also be what makes the director capable of understanding what people are seeking in and through the concrete particulars of their everyday life.

Neither spiritual director nor directee need to be mystics or experts in religious experiencing. Although religious experiencing is a universal fact found in all great religious traditions, some people definitely have a greater capacity for this kind of experience than others. It is clear that persons from certain nationalities, backgrounds, training and even temperament, are more sensitive to the religious or mystical dimension of experience than others. Capacity for experience of any kind, be it mystical or merely mundane, is not the center of spiritual life. For Christians who accept the Biblical tradition, the central domain is no longer that of religious experience, but of faith. It is faith in Christ that is the center of spiritual life — the faith that leads the person to do the will of God, to surrender his or her life in adherence to His revealed word. Christ tells us that faith, not experience, is what introduces the person into participation in the life of God. Faith is what brings us in touch with God's initiative towards us. It is ultimately God's gift. An appreciative sense of the possibility of experiential breakthrough to the divine should also be noted by the director so that he or she may appraise the authentic power of these "experiences" in the person who seeks to be open to the Holy Spirit in his or her life.

Connection of baptism with mission

Experiential realization of one's being personally caught up in the divine economy at Baptism does not happen to us all at once. Even in the primitive Christian communities, we have evidence from the Epistles that the seed of faith planted in Baptism needed time to grow and develop. The wisdom God gave to understand the Mystery, the plan he was pleased to decree in Christ[13] met then, as it does now, a whole series of barriers in the form of personal, psychological blockages, and societal customs that closed hearts off from recognizing and uniting with the "already there" life of grace. Once men and women were baptized, they entered into a larger reality, into the body of Christ. Contemplative realization of the working of God's Spirit in that body carried with it a growing sense of being loved and chosen by God, as well as a sense of personal responsibility for active participation in the growth and development of the world. Just as there was recognition of a mysterious divine direction underlying the larger whole, so too each baptized Christian was called to discover a corresponding divine direction or mission underlying his or her particular life. Spiritual direction was concerned then, as it is now, primarily with the hidden orientation or directedness towards the Mystery that is present in the core of each person's being and that corresponds with his or her unique spiritual identity or calling,[14] as a member of the Body of Christ.

Actually, a discovery and incarnation of this hidden directedness is the main focus of spiritual direction in most great spiritual traditions. However, its roots for traditions that find their basic revelation of the nature of the Real in the Old and New Testaments of the Bible, reach back to the moment when the all encompassing Being spoke to a group of nomads in the desert telling them I AM.[15] They felt called as a people by this Divine Being to live a transformed life, although it took them years of attempts and failures to learn what that call would mean in terms of their actual daily life. Throughout the Old Testament we find event upon event of God's being with his people (immanence) as well as a quality of distinct otherness or transcendence that incorporates a sense of mission and a demand for performance. The people of God are to transform their hearts in relation to this mysterious calling; they are also expected to put that transformation into practice in loving service to others. They are to go out of themselves into the world, each in his or her unique fashion to discover ways of incarnating the attitudes they have learned in their relation with the Holy Other. In the New Testament this pattern is repeated as Jesus tells his followers to unite themselves first of all to him, as the branch is united to the vine, and then to go forth and bear plentiful fruit in lives of love for others.[16]

For contemporary Christians, this mixture of contemplation of the Mystery and active ministry in the world is the means by which they will gradually discover the hidden direction that each one most deeply is. Both the contemplative or mystical dimension and the more situated or incarnate are part of the directee's positive experienc of being drawn into union with the Holy. Every human being also experiences negative feelings and possible fear or anxiety on account of the sheer immensity and uncontrollability of this Holy Other and the difficulty of his demands. Awe can easily turn into anxiety when the finite human person finds himself powerless, vulnerable and dependent on a terrifying Beyond,[17] whose call is a challenge to new and sometimes disturbing experiences of growth and change.

Much more could be said about this demand quality of the Holy Other who is also a loving God. The important point for the Christian spiritual director lies in the recognition that when direction involves the person's call or begins to deal with concrete details of the directees' ministry or mission in the world, it is necessary to make the connection between the transcendent and challenging Other and the immanent nearness who calls each unique person out of isolation into intimacy as a son or daughter in the family of the Trinity.

Self-knowledge in spiritual direction

Men and women who have begun to perceive reality within the horizon of the Mystery described in Paul's letter to the Ephesians seek to discern the meaning of their life choices and actions in light of the broader plan of salvation willed by the Father. Desiring gradually to grow in presence to that mystery, they realize that such growth brings with it more self-knowledge. As they awaken to a new way of seeing God as the initiator of their spiritual life, whose gratuitous loving presence cannot be grasped or controlled by man, they must take a fresh look at themselves also. The spiritual director in this sense may also have to help the person from a psychological point of view. He will find that most people are unaware of the obstacles they tend to put in the way of God's initiatives towards them. Also their knowledge of themselves is based primarily on the exterior identity they have picked up from family, friends, and a lifetime's practice of filling societal roles based on other people's expectations. Most of us simply do not recognize the particular ways in which we close ourselves off from the Holy, via these alienating roles and expectations.

Paul's new man, the "pneumatized"[18] person who is the subject of Christian spiritual direction, has undertaken a radical change in his manner of being, seeing and living; he must be aware of himself always in relation to the Mystery, as a being fundamentally known and loved by God, and not merely as an isolated empirical self. It is the responsibility of the spiritual director to make sure that this kind of self-knowledge is the ground of the directee's growing appreciation of himself. He shows the directee the difference between the relatively isolated self-knowledge that results from a merely psychological approach to self-awareness by means of introspection, and the knowledge of self-in-relation-to-Mystery that comes with meditative reflection on that same self as loved by God. The latter approach does not deny limitations, sinfulness, imperfections and errors, but it avoids the despair that may attend isolated focusing on the problematics of one's irrevocable past with its misdeeds and hang-ups, its accumulation of guilt and its sense of waste.[19] Despair is often a real accompaniment of growth in self-knowledge in the therapeutic counseling situation, whereas in spiritual direction this same helplessness points to one's hope in divine redemption.

Spiritual direction is grounded in awakening to the authentic presence of the God of Mystery on whose transcending initiative human existence depends. The possibility of coming to a knowledge of self that is true and fundamental seems more sure somehow in this process even though its results can never be measured or tested. Christian spiritual leaders need to know and respect the dynamics of human growth and development as set forth in the psychological sciences; they ought to be able to judge when a particular person is in need of strictly therapeutic counseling rather than spiritual direction. In general, however, the transformation aimed at either through the reorientation of one's thinking and action as in therapy, or even through education and enlightment as in Eastern religious traditions, is often antithetical to the transformation aimed at by spiritual direction. For instance, one of the usual aims of therapy is to bring a non-functioning, inefficient person to the point where he or she can begin to function efficiently once again. Later, in spiritual direction, this same efficiently functioning person may feel called to surrender a little of that pragmatic functional efficiency so that the spiritual dimension of his or her being may come to the fore. In due time, the person who has undergone a radical spiritual reorientation is likely to be even more efficient in serving the needs of others, though his style of doing so will be marked by a relaxed open manner of one who no longer clings to willful control of his or her life.

In this transformation, we see that the person's consciousness as well as will has been reoriented in the direction of surrender to the will of God. The metanoia aimed at in spiritual direction is not simply a change of one's mind or consciousness, but a surrender of one's whole person, a surrender achieved often at great cost to one's "natural" ways of thinking and willing. Love of God, actively witnessed to in love for neighbor, is what matters for the individual heart that begins to find its unique call in the Holy Spirit by means of traditional Christian spiritual direction.

CHAPTER VII

THE PARTICULAR INDIVIDUAL WHO COMES

Basically healthy and free

For Jesus, the apostles and the Fathers, people from the crowds who came seeking direction were never simply typical members of "the masses." From the earliest time we notice that each person is respected as a unique individual with his or her own personal style of hearing and understanding the message. We notice also that all spiritual direction dialogues, up to and including the present, seem to require a serious attempt to perceive each directee in all his or her particularity as "this" concrete, original, situated yet basically free member of the human race. Possibly we touch here on a source of increasing perplexity for contemporary spiritual guides who, due to the twentieth century explosion of knowledge via the human sciences, are able to be so much more aware than were spiritual directors of the past, of all that lies within each person who comes for direction in the way of both limitation and freedom.

Today disciplines like psychology, psychiatry, sociology and anthropology have given names to much of the intricate complexity that marks human existence. As themselves products of this scientific age, directors are likely to feel at times overwhelmed by the findings of a discipline like psychology, forgetting that along side of a 2,000 year-old discipline like Christian spiritual direction, psychology is still in its infancy. Impressed and perhaps even discouraged by the flood of literature about the human person produced by empirical scientists, those entrusted with the spiritual direction task may not realize that much of what these scientists are pointing to as "new information" has been assumed in the richness of the great religious traditions of the world for centuries. There is, however, much that can be learned by spiritual directors who will listen respectfully to the ways in which contemporary therapists and social scientists describe those who come to consult them. These are, after all, the same men and women who at some time in their lives may seek spiritual direction.

Familiarity with the thinking of more psychologically oriented counselors will also be of help when the director has to decide whether spiritual direction or psychological counseling, or perhaps a mixture of both, is called for in particular instances. For example, a great many people today are experiencing a loss of freedom, a sense of being restricted, impeded, trapped and closed off from a natural and fulfilling dialogue with the persons, things and events of their world. One of their hopes for restoration of that lost freedom lies in seeking out teachers, therapists, friends, guides, counselors or directors who seem to be living a less anxious, more integrated and satisfying life of dialogue with reality and who are willing to be with them in their attempts to change. We find men, women and even children from all walks of life describing their paralyzed anxious existence in more or less psychological terminology. They complain of not being in touch or at home with their own bodies, with themselves, with other people, and/or with the larger world of cultural and natural reality. They speak of "losing control," of "having a breakdown," of "being alienated" from self or others; they say they have come to be healed of "loneliness" and "isolation." Are these people looking for a therapist or a spiritual director? Obviously, psychological insights comprise a necessary dimension of one's recognition of partial ways in which the basic spiritual freedom of the person who comes may be restricted. In view of the fact that the spiritual director cannot afford to be ignorant of how the psychotherapist tends to perceive human beings, this chapter will focus on some of the ways in which psychologists describe the particular individual who comes.[1]

Towards the end of Chapter 3 we noted that one type of therapist will see freedom as restricted by such classic "neurotic problems" as ego loss; fixation in infantile modes; hysterical or obsessional patterns of behavior; schizoid separation from reality; or failure to adjust. Another sees the person's inability to achieve goals of self-actualization and interpersonal relationships as defining his loss of freedom. In addition, if the person has been obviously jolted out of his taken-for-granted world by the sudden death of someone close, by sickness, loss of income or reputation, by a divorce or some other deprivation of what has become familiar and thus necessary for well-being, a therapist in touch with the invisible ground of these problematic "appearances" might realize that the person's anxiety refers not only to the problem he has but to the deeper mystery he is. It is the rare therapist who is prepared to deal with the person whose presenting anxiety refers to questions about the meaning of his or her seemingly gratifying life; who simply wants to know whether this is "all there is," whose whole living soul cries out for a horizon of meaning that will satisfy his potential for relationship with Holy. Incidentally, it may be the equally rare spiritual director who is able and willing to step back into a prerevealed psychologically-oriented point of view of the human person that touches at its source the movement from illusion towards freedom as it is experienced by anxious suffering people and those who are their counselors.

How do contemporary psychologists view the normally

neurotic[2] person in our divided society? Until the second half of the twentieth century, it seemed as if most psychologists took it for granted that the human person was determined by his situatedness and was, therefore, an "object" for the natural sciences to scrutinize. Yet already in the nineteenth century there had emerged the phenomenological movement,[3] a way of seeing that described the human being as "situated *freedom,*" as incarnated spirit or finiteness longing for infinity. This view, adopted by an increasing number of psychologists, psychoanalysts and even sociologists, sees the person as a determined yet at the same time somewhat free intentional relation with the world of reality as it presents itself in the form of people, events and things.

Briefly, the person is seen as a self-determining, purposeful reactive/response to this world, an openness to its vital, personal and spiritual meaning. As possibility of transcendence into the world, the person, according to this view, emerges in dialogue with his temperament, his intellectual-functional capacity, and his natural spirit. In a society such as ours where vital and functional meanings predominate, it is logical to judge that the vast majority of men and women operates according to horizontal or vital/functional modes of being and relating. These thinkers point out that because of a certain repression of spiritual meaning in our world, most contemporary persons, whether they recognize it or not, are undergoing a like concealment of the spiritual dimension of their being.[4] This closed world view of our society is regarded by them as a major limitation of truly human freedom.

They also point out that when persons from our society with their neurotic problems come to consult a therapist, they will probably present their difficulties and symptoms in terms of the horizontal meanings common to our socie-

ty. If the counselor or teacher is not reflectively present to
the ground from which these partial appearances emerge,
he or she will also tend to speak from the natural attitude
of embeddedness in merely pragmatic meanings. They
conclude that the therapist whose consciousness is also
structured by the society in which she and the client live
will probably not be able to see the underlying invisible
hope of transcendence that lies beneath the obvious visible
problems of functioning and development that the person
seems to have; she will not be able to act beyond what she
sees.

According to this phenomenological approach, persons
who come for counseling can be seen as emerging, flowing, changing fields of consciousness; as embodied relationships of knowing, willing and feeling. These persons
will tend to perceive their world as a highly idiosyncratic
mixture of ideas, concepts, objects, events, nature, people
and things. Because they are always conscious of a changing world of meaning, they themselves are also always
changing; they give new meaning to their experience of
that world and to that unique stream of life of which they
are the living context. Such clients appear to a therapist as
unique worlds of personal meanings set against the larger
socio-economic context of their shared world. When these
clients enter the consulting room, they bring with them the
many worlds of meaning that correspond to relationships
they have with various parts of the whole. That is, they
bring their world of family relations, work, recreation,
reading and music; of fears, love, interests, hobbies; of
fantasy and self-understanding. They also bring their lack
of relationship with these worlds of meaning. It is the
therapist's task to notice a break in the client's dialogue
with a family member; a lack of interest in his or her
work; an absence of recreation; a difficulty in aesthetic

appreciation; a dearth of love or interest; an alienation from others or themselves. Phenomenologically-oriented therapists will probably describe the person who comes as one who is fixated on the level of vital meanings, able to react mainly from a prereflective stance towards predominantly organismic values and meanings of persons, events and things, or as one who is caught on the level of pragmatic ego-level attentiveness to things, people and events, perceiving them only in their meaning as predictable and controllable by him. The therapist gradually begins to understand the points at which the client's relationships with possible worlds of meaning are truncated or closed off, and moves to help the client restructure those relationships.

Of primary interest to the spiritual director in all this is the fact that certain therapists experience the human person not only as a structured, statically situated presence but also simultaneously as a transcending possibility of being restructured or changed; they genuinely believe in the possibility of real change as the goal of the therapeutic encounter. These therapists realize that the person who feels miserable and trapped by past encounters and distorted relationships, who believes that reality is exactly as he perceived it, seeks dialogue with them out of a negative anxious experience of his dialogue with the world. Tending to see themselves and their life as constituted by others, by the past, by situations that are beyond their control, clients look to the therapist for help in understanding and coping with what has gone wrong. Usually they do not see beyond the immediately perceptible "trouble" that overwhelms them.

What the therapist has to work with is the clients' potential for going beyond immediacy, for transcending the closed circuit of reaction to stimuli they have become, for reflecting or bending back on their experience from a different, broader point of view. This healthy potential for freedom, for becoming aware in a new way of one's experience and its meaning, that is, for becoming the constituting subject of one's actions and experience rather than merely remaining a constituted object, is central to the restructuration or change that takes place in therapeutic situations where the therapist is respectfully present to the other as fundamentally healthy and free. The same might be said for the spiritual director who is called upon first of all to believe in whatever limited freedom may be present in the other, and secondly, to count on that freedom as the natural foundation for change.

Socially conditioned and defensive

Taking into account this contemporary psychological approach to human freedom, we now turn to the way some therapists are currently approaching the question of determinism, or "situatedness." What questions surround the more or less unfree, limiting or given elements involved in being human?[5] In the light of this approach, to be born means to become embodied, not only in a given, genetically determined constellation of biological, organic and psychological facts, but also in an equally given "second body," composed primarily of family, cultural, societal and racial inheritance. According to this theory, throughout the whole of each person's life it is necessary to acknowledge the "facticity" of his or her socio-economic, cultural, aesthetic and/or national and religious horizons in all their narrowness and limitation as well as in the positive contribution they make towards his or her project of existence.[6] There is no escaping the fact that we are born into a certain point of view about "the way things are." This consciousness is transmitted to us by others before we consciously choose it as orienting our personal directedness towards the world. The social dimension of our existence, the early constitution of our social and personal identity, is seen by many theorists as a factor contributing both to the person's sense of self and also to his loss of this sense or self-alienation. In other words, it is through what our family, teachers and other members of society tell us, that we find out who we are; what roles we are expected to play; what our meaning is as a member of a particular family, nation, ethnic group or race; as a participant in a particular political, professional or religious grouping.

This sense of the self[7] is further constituted by a history of personal choices within this plurality of possible worlds of meaning and by a certain sense of deciding on directions and relationships that are "me" rather than "not me." Already from their earliest years most people have sensed dimly the impossibility of always choosing to do and be what coincides with who they really are in the face of contradictory demands of "the others" whose approval and/or respect they need and want. For the majority of persons in our society, this tension emerges in the form of a sense of personal identity that, due to its co-constitution by society in general and significant others in particular, has lost touch with its unique originality, with its deepest direction. Thus, persons who come for therapy, or for spiritual direction, may well have lost touch with their actual spontaneous selves; they may be unable to see beyond the stresses and strains that have become problematic for their pragmatic ego. It is also possible that both the vital and the spiritual dimensions of their self-identity and of the worlds of meaning they can potentially inhabit, have been lost or distorted. They no longer see either themselves or the world as a connected whole. They are trapped in a horizontal perspective. They are in need, as a phenomeno-logically-oriented psychologist might say, of a restructur-ation of consciousness in order to be free to discover the truth of who they really are.

Another way of looking at the loss of freedom or self that accompanies the gradual substitution of a social reac-tive pattern or ego-identity for one's unique originality, lies in seeing how the human person tends to lock himself into a defensive character armor originating in spiritual rather than social anxiety.[8] Evidently the helpless child, confronted by the beauty, majesty and terror of All That Is, can be driven by anxiety to deny or repress the "too-muchness" of reality, and then to become defensively dis-honest about himself and his situation. In order to have the illusion of psychological security and control, of power and status, the human being tends to substitute "lit-tle beyonds" and a falsely consistent self system for the great Beyond and the unpredictable risks of an open- end-ed spiritual life. The person's rigid and programmed sense of self, his or her relatively unchangeable "character," is thus seen by these therapists as a mask concealing the paradox of the human condition, as a repression of the restlessness for "more" that truly characterizes the situated human spirit. They must deal with the ways that the illusion of being safe, secure and in control is further bolstered by clinging to attachments, first to one's mother and all the familiar embedded attitudes of childhood; then to certain self enhancing possessions and positions; to comfortable ideas and even obsessions; and to a style and project of life that one can manage and control. Clearly they are pointing to areas of concern for the spiritual director as well.

Actually, both therapists and directors would hold that most people who experience acute anxiety regarding their own vulnerability and limitation are not free enough even to consider moving out of their fixation in partial wholes or objects of attachment to assimilate new meanings in a broader horizon. Yet the path to liberation, whether in therapy or direction, seems to lie precisely along the lines of letting go of falsely consistent life patterns — of closely guarded investment in the little beyonds of social relevance and driven, anxious embeddedness in somewhat neurotic illusions about what constitutes an acceptable human life style. Usually the person in therapy puts the problem in terms of what might happen or of what should or should not happen, implying that all he or she needs to learn is how to control things, to be able to manage their own destiny, and then all will be well. It is as hard for the client in therapy as for the person in spiritual direction to see that an overemphasis on ego values and assumptions is exactly what has produced much of the anxiety they are already experiencing; a broadening of the horizon in which they see these realities would help considerably in liberating them from the narrow oppression of spirit in which they now live.

Lacking a sense of self-identity

One area to which psychologists give a great deal of attention is that of identity, of the client's sense of self. In fact, it is often a crisis having to do with threats to the freedom to be one's self that impells people to "go into therapy" in the first place. Yet in our society, we are realizing that this particular crisis is not easily recognized. It is perhaps easier to see and diagnose a behavioral or psychological maladjustment or problem than to tune in to what certain thinkers now identify as the malaise of the spirit, a restlessness or fixation in the "natural attitude" that is at the root of much suffering among contemporary men and women.[9]

Traditional therapists are more or less prepared to deal with the obviously hysterical personality and its attention-getting maneuvers; with the obsessive-compulsive style and its rigid, indecisive concerns; or with the depressive syndrome and its hidden anger and helplessness. All of them are familiar with resistant clients who need to maintain their repression and defend their right to remain unfree, and with reluctant clients who never chose the counseling situation in the first place. It is not so difficult to recognize specifically developmental crises either, when people need to talk about moving from one stage of life to the next. There are typical problems that belong to adolescence or young married life or to those approaching the middle years or old age.[10] But the possibility of coming to grips with one's false identity, with the nature of one's deepest self, seems to have become even more obscured by some of the taken-for-granted explanations offered by our society for why the person seeking help is caught in an uncongenial life style[11] in the first place. Traditionally, the whole responsibility for self-alienation is placed on the person's past.

Certainly each person is a temporal synthesis of past, present and future orientations, and past encounters with others, as non-traditional thinkers would readily admit, have a great deal to do with one's basic sense of the world. Phenomenologically-oriented psychologists would say that the lived intentionality, the vital predisposition that each one is, was co-constituted by the emotional atmosphere of his or her past object-relations, and that to ignore or try to crush this inner child of the past can be in itself

self-alienating. They would even add that attempting to be one's own parent in reaction to past attitudes can also distort one's relation to oneself, as can preoccupation with "unfinished business' from past situations or relationships. Our perception and thus our experience of present persons, events and things is colored by past experience or lack of experience of similar realities, and an impoverished past lacking enriching experiences or characterized by fear of acknowledging certain aspects of one's given reality, can make for a present self that is impoverished because worthless and unloved. It is also true, they would agree, that the developmental dynamics of most of us have been interrupted from time to time by stresses from the environment and by frustration of inner needs and strivings in the past. Some persons find themselves fixated at early stages of development, unfree to allow the risks of growth. Finally the danger of losing one's identity and unique life direction in the pressure to conform to the expectations and models set forth by others in the past would be acknowledged by these therapists along with the difficulties and self-doubt experienced by the person who tries to resist these pressures.

However, from the earliest years there also survives in every human existence some marginal possibility for transcendence, for going beyond what is merely given, for not totally surrendering to what others or the culture would have us be or do. No one is simply the sum of his or her past encounters; we are also always a synthesis of present reality and future protentions.[12] At a certain point there is in all of us this small spark of freedom, this repressed recognition of oneself as also spirit encapsulated in an alien and divided self. This spark can be enkindled; it can awaken from its long sleep. The occasion of the awakening may, and often does, according to these theorists, come from outside the self in a "limit situation."[13] This refers to a personally significant interruption or even disruption of our taken-for-granted routine and the accustomed ways we have developed to deal with it. These more or less jolting situations range on a continuum from major cataclysms like war or natural disasters involving many perons in an abrupt awakening from the unquestioning security of the sleep of the everyday; through personal situations of loss such as sudden death, retirement, divorce, oncoming middle or old age, sickness or disability, unemployment or unexpected poverty and failure; to small, almost insignificant anxieties that arise within the unpredictableness of daily life relationships. Often it is the very narrowness of the daily space/time context or situation itself that gives rise to a certain sense of uneasiness, to a self-reflective questioning or a disquieting discovery that all is not well with oneself and one's world.

What are the possible consequences of being thus forced to "stop and think," to become aware of our unease, discomfort, restlessness, boredom and frustration, of our lack of at-homeness in a formerly complacent, sleepy existence? Contemporary psychologists note that persons may attempt to regain their former familiarity in the world by means of simple substitution of other persons, things or activities for what has been lost. They also see the possibility of a more reflective decision in the face of this personal or social abyss that has opened in life. One may choose to pursue the meaning of this dismaying experience, somehow to come to grips with it as a part of the whole that is one's life, to seek not substitution and a return to the past, but rather change and movement into the future. This more reflective approach might involve some form of introspective self-searching seen as a more or less disciplined bending back on experience by means of thoughtful presence to the hitherto undiscovered self. It might include keeping a journal; discussing anxious or alienated feelings with a friend; or turning to self-help books, lectures, or techniques of religious meditation; it may also result in seeking out a therapist and entering into a contractual dialogue as has alreay been described.

Whatever means are chosen for coping with this crisis, they are always accompanied by feelings of uncertainty and risk as well as hope and positive expectation, because the person is somehow pre-reflectively aware that he or she is facing the unfamiliar, the unknown. Temporarily out of touch with self, persons who come for therapy may not consciously be aware that their real identity has somehow been hidden under a false identity or mask that will have to be gradually removed. They will probably not realize concretely the loss of freedom entailed in the narcissistic projections, illusions, and self-paralysis that have resulted from leading a defensive, ego-controlling life. Probably such persons will not recognize the restrictions placed on their existence by ignorance and miseducation of self, by an unbalanced imposition of what some therapists call ego or superego illusions. These persons who come both know and do not know that one way of describing their crisis might be to call it a crisis of self- identity. They have substituted a false self for the true self, and are living in the unfreedom of illusion. Yet all therapists know that somehow these persons sense that this process of moving back into touch with themselves can be a slow and painful one, involving both anxiety and risk. Thus, the first consultation is usually quite an ordeal.

The therapist has first of all to be aware of this anxiety on the part of the client, and to appreciate the courage manifested in having made the decision to come. He or she must also have a sensitive respect for the other's freedom and dignity and for the infinite and unknown possibilities of self-emergence that each client is. Actually there are many fine volumes about counselor attitudes and techniques, with which it would be well for the spiritual director to become familiar, since much of the above applies to his or her beginning sessions as well. What I want to do now is to point to some areas of self-discovery common in the practice of therapy. Persons called to assist others in discovering their spiritual direction may learn from these examples. At the very least spiritual directors need to be able to recognize self-alienation and its sources in our society. A director must also have a sense of when the directee's psychological needs are beyond his or her competence, and when a referral to a psychotherapist should be made.

Tending towards illusion and encapsulation

Most therapists would agree that the persons they see in therapy usually lack self-awareness because they are caught in a conflict between their actual self and the ideal self their ego has projected of the person they ought to be. Whether to gain the approval of others or to live up to unrealistic standards they themselves have set, such persons have divided themselves into the acknowledged self and the unacknowledged self, the "me" and the "not me," the self I aim to be and the self I actually am. Such a split in the self is at the basis of much neurotic anxiety. It forces the person to cling not only to an unreal, supposedly "higher" self, but also to ignore, suppress or deny a real, somewhat limited and therefore "lower" self. This projected ideal self was originally and partially constructed from values originating in others and society; it will thus always be somewhat alien to the uniqueness of the true, inner self of the person, and will probably reflect values currently alive in that society. For example, many young people in the '60's in North America lost touch with themselves by trying to be idealized "hippies," whereas in the '50's and the '70's just as many may have become the self-alienated, idealized "successful executive" type. Persons in the perfectionistic society of certain religious groups may lose touch with themselves by becoming a "model of virtue" for others, while persons in a competitive group or family may become self-alienated by totalizing the striving self at the expense of their relaxed, carefree side.

Obviously there are any number of ways in which human beings can become forgetful of and need to rediscover lost areas of themselves, be they in the form of disturbing limitations or of ignored possibilities that have been thrust aside in favor of projecting the ideal image. Thus, the "model of virtue" may have to accept his own vital needs, drives and sensations, as well as his not so virtuous anger and selfishness. Indeed it may have been the unexpected erruption of irrational likes and dislikes that brought him to counseling in the first place.

I remember one person who had embraced a hippie identity in the '60's telling me of being shocked into re-identification with his functional self when no one in his drugged group of friends was willing or able to get up and fix a broken window that was letting cold air flow in on all of them. On the other hand, a successful executive may suddenly feel he needs professional help when his functional self lets him down, or his hypertension gets out of hand. In the course of counseling he may discover that he is not only the loving, tender husband and father he had forgotten about in his life of striving, but also that there reside in him hesitant, awkward desires for a more spiritual existence. These were repressed in his outer world of business and, as a consequence, in his inner world of self as well. Perhaps as his shift towards meditative self-presence[14] progresses under the guidance of the counselor, he will move beyond preoccupation with negative experiences and actually begin to be interested in their invisible sacred ground. It is almost impossible, once persons begin seriously to uncover and try to deal with their alienated sides, to avoid admitting the fundamentally spiritual nature of human selfhood. This is precisely the point at which some more traditional therapists and counselors are not able or willing to be of further assistance to their clients.

Therapists agree that we can trace the need for a false self identity, with its defensive style of coping with reality, back to basic anxiety we experienced as powerless, vulnerable children whose desire for safety and security impelled us to gain control over the love and approval we would earn from others. They also agree that the resultant splitting of the self has profoundly alienated parts of the total organism of most persons from an alive contact with corresponding aspects of the world. For example, we find adults whose divorce from their current emotional life was precipitated by an anxious desire to avoid experiencing painful disagreements that may have permeated their childhood home life. Thus, many neurotic persons are alienated from their bodily presence to reality. They ignore signals from their body in its interaction with the world and are almost unaware of their emotions or feelings. They allow themselves to live only "out of their minds" because their earthly, grounded aliveness does not fit well with their disembodied ideal self-image. Accompanying this loss of the spontaneous flow of feelings and vital energy is a fixation in which the person becomes rigidly confined to reacting in terms of the role or "character" demanded by an idealized, societally-constituted image.

The counseling process must help overcome this anxious self-alienated condition by putting persons in touch once again with their spontaneous feelings, with their sexual likes and dislikes, and by pointing to and if possible eliminating some of the tyrannical "shoulds"[15] of the idealized self from their lives. Only then may they more freely respond to the persons, things and events that make up the call of reality for them. Much therapy aims at a reunification of the conflicted yet always emerging self, so that there is a better balance of the vital-personal reaction and response. Few therapists countenance an overbalance in the direction of gratifying the vital self, however; the "reality principle" keeps the flow of vital energy channeled so that the aims of society are achieved.

The interesting point here is that few therapists in contemporary North American society seem to object to what may be a gross overbalance in the direction of fostering the horizontal ego-controlling dimensions of the self. Only gradually are they beginning to discover that contemporary people are tense and neurotic, not so much because of a totalization of sexual needs, but because they have become fixated on what one writer calls "intermediate wholes."[16] They have totalized their work and activity, their social relations, individual preferences, or aesthetic likes and dislikes to such an extent that most of their vital energy is tied up in what he calls functionalism, social activism, individualism and aestheticism. Finding their complete identify in their role as contributor to society in a certain profession or service capacity, in having a socially relevant effect on their own or another culture, in becoming a recognized personality or even character, or in making an exclusive idol of some aspect of goodness, truth or beauty, can reduce the whole person to one totalized part of life.[17]

It is at this point that the contemporary therapist must be more capable than most are of sensitively and respectfully recognizing that the client who may appear to be fully normal and to have his more vivid infantile modes under the control of his adult self, is not yet a whole person, despite the fact that he or she is functioning well as father or mother, doctor, lawyer, artist, etc.

In my opinion, the therapist, from her wider perspective on reality, must be convinced that being a whole person does not mean simply having the ability to do or accomplish these otherwise worthy and needed contributions to society. She must be aware that pouring oneself into one's family, into care of one's health, into the study of music or science, into being well liked and admired, or even into being the leader of a religious group can, if totalized, merely provide the person with a substitute for his true identity, for such a totalization on the personal level often excludes other levels of human wholeness.

Yet, because our society encourages and rewards such one-sided dedication, it is not easy for therapists to resist this pressure. Fortunately more and more thinkers are now discovering that persons whose identities are thus focused and confined to the level of ego-control and accomplishment, are often locked into a neurotic overall life style that remains inflexible and closed not only to vital but to spiritual influences as well. Actually, spiritual directors have always known that such persons have made a "religion" of "little beyonds" like their work, their ideas, their family, their personal development or even their devotional life, and in so doing, have been mainly defending themselves against the anxiety of being open to the

Great Beyond. It is no secret to someone aware of the real depth and richness of the spiritual life, that these persons have encapsulated themselves in an illusion that has the appearance of being a full and rich life. Their somewhat inflexible or compulsive life style, their barely hidden fanatical pursuit of success in those chosen and limited worlds of meaning, their somewhat hysterical or obsessive one-sidedness, actually betrays an absence of relaxed faithful living, as well as repression of the truly human and spiritual dimensions of their lives. This encapsulation is simply one more example of how ordinary human problems can become obstacles to the life of the spirit.

Unless such encapsulated persons are somehow awakened to their own inner longing for "something more," they will never be considered abnormal or even be advised to seek counseling. They fit only too well into our contemporary "normal madness,"[18] into our alienated concensus and collective illusion about the way things are. Reinforced in this narrow, almost pathological perception of what it means to be human, many contemporary men and women (including some counselors) are unaware of how impoverished their lives have become, how alienated they are from the whole of All That Is, and from their deepest selves as well. Whether they tend to find their ultimate security in fragmentary finite satisfactions like comfort, popularity and power, or whether they have widened their self-encapsulation to include larger, even internationally acclaimed functional enterprises, these one-dimensional universes continue to exclude openness to meanings that come from Beyond and that provide the ground against which true identity can be revealed and understood. Unless the therapist bases her understanding of the human person on a similarly open-ended ground or context, it is doubtful that clients can hope to deal adequately with alienated aspects of the self. On what other basis does a counselor of any kind confront the client's illusions and projections? In what light does she clarify and/or interpret them? For what greater goal does she encourage the other to work them through and finally to abandon them for better modes of being in the world? The fact remains that an increasing number of therapeutic counselors are becoming disillusioned with the patterns for wholeness and self-understanding handed on by the psychological ego establishment of our society. Merely vital, personal, functional, social, scientific or aesthetic ideals are no longer as compelling as they may have been in the past. Excellent as these ideals are, and necessary as they still must be if we are to progress at all as a civilization and a people, many men and women are now asking for more.

They sense that they were created for more than simply identifying themselves with their "doing," no matter how necessary and laudable. They feel victimized by an inner driveness to keep doing something, not to waste time in "useless pursuits," to become successful in ways society deems relevant — all of which seems to be in conflict with a deeper message they cannot quite name. They begin to sense that counselors, lecturers, and self-help books, which remain only within the horizon of immediate personal and societal meanings, are inadequate. They dislike finding themselves perceiving people, events and things in their life with the alienating eyes of envious comparison and competition, or as inconvenient impingements on their life space and time. They are no longer satisfied with hiding their restlessness and uneasiness beneath compensatory substitutes for the wild richness and beauty of reality. They are beginning to be challenged by the unsatisfactory nature of the illusions to which they cling, of the self-alienation that is theirs. They want to be done with the dependent, immature existence they glimpsed in moments of being jolted out of their complacency. They want to go beyond where they are living now; they seek out another who can help them get in touch with who they most truly are and will become in the future. In the meantime, they find themselves clinging to the attachments of the false self, to dependency, possessiveness, fears, anxieties, obsessions and willfulness, because they are unaware of what it is that could satisfy their whole self. They know only that they find themselves having to retain tight control over their lives and destinies. Prisoners of their own narrowed perception of what is and what should be, they may also be victims of the too narrow perspectives of the very people who are trying to help them. In fact, it is often the therapist who must be helped to recognize the need to refer her client to a spiritual director.

Having problems with interpersonal relations

Even a psychologically unsophistocated spiritual director senses when something has changed or gone awry in her relation with the directee. The other seems to be over-reacting, making an increasing number of demands for time or attention or becoming unexpectedly negative or positive in the interaction. Signs of over-dependence, like notes and phone calls between sessions or a strong attempt to put the relationship on an informal friendship basis, may begin to appear.

All therapists are familiar with these manifestations of lack of balance in the person's relatedness with another person. An increasing number recognize the centrality for therapy of these interpersonal patterns of relating that belong to the client's human condition of being in the world with others. In our century at least, the social reality of others, the ramifications of being one of the "lonely crowd," is simply a given in life. In fact many psychiatrists[19] find the psycho-social success or failure of their clients to be of primary importance — more central than any other aspect of the client's dialogue with reality.

From my own experience as a psychologist, I would say that clients seem to present many of the problem areas of their lives in terms of their relations with other people, either with significant others from the past (usually parents and other authority figures) or with those whose lives touch theirs in the present (spouses, children, parents, work and social contacts).

Not only are people in our culture acutely aware of themselves as relating to others in ways that are comfortable or uncomfortable, normal or abnormal, but they are often either dimly or sharply aware of their lack of relation with what we might call the social or interpersonal dimensions of the world. Thus, clients speak of their loneliness, of their not being accepted or understood, of their feelings of isolation and personal distance from members of their family, group or society. They describe unsuccessful attempts to bridge these relational gaps, or the fears that prevent them from trying. Some wonder how they can improve their personality and become more worthwhile in the eyes of colleagues, friends, children, spouses, while others would prefer to learn how to keep the other at a still safer distance by improved methods of prediction and control.

In the midst of all these contradictions, there seem to be some universally accepted underlying assumptions about the tremendous importance of interpersonal relatedness in our culture. Against the horizon of these implicit societal meanings, the human person is given to understand from the beginning that how one relates to others, how they accept or do not accept him and his need to come to terms with the web of relationships that he is, must be given a high priority in life.

In spite of the obvious social nature of the human condition, with its deep substructure of interwoveness with all other members of the human race and its universal tendency towards homonomy[20] or belonging, it is not surprising to find that from the beginning of human societies there has been a sense both of the sameness we all share as human beings, and of the embodied differences that separate us from each other. Inevitably each man and woman, by the very fact of having been born a unique constellation of biological, organic, metabolic, temperamental and psychological directedness towards the world, becomes conscious at some point in life, of his or her difference from all "others." Possibilities for separation are further emphasized when somewhat prejudiced ways of perceiving and acting, based on the traditions, customs and mentality of one's family, clash with the perceptual and actional patterns of others. For many, the time of growing up is confusing largely because of this tension between a natural desire to find oneself as belonging in society with others and the equally strong desire to find oneself as different from others, as unique. Much has been written, not only in comtemporary psychiatry but also in literature, theology and philosophy, about the estrangement from others experienced by human beings whose failure to attain a feeling of communion with their fellows is attributed to various socio-economic, political, ideological and sociological causes and/or to the more introspective and socially unacceptable tendencies of a culture where analytic, utilitarian examinations of self and society are encouraged.[21]

Whatever may be the reasons behind it, I think it is safe to say that many people in our particular generation have either been conditioned by the culture or moved to make decisions out of their own anxious need to cut themselves off from humanly energizing relations with their world. Retired within a shell whose outer manifestation may simply be boredom, discontent or dissatisfaction, these persons fall back on themselves. The world of other persons loses its power to call them forth. They short-circuit their connection with others and the flow of energy between them is cut off, sometimes permanently. Cut off also is the interest the world of other persons may have held for them. They are no longer attentive to the richness and variety that comprises the horizon of others' lives. Figural only are ways of controlling the unpredictableness of these others so that they do not infringe upon the fixed and rigid "character" this lonely person presents to the world.

Again we come up against the theme of basic anxiety that lies at the origin of this unfree, inflexible consistency described earlier as "character." As I noted then, one's character armor or "fortress self"[22] is not seen by all theorists as simply a product of so-called social anxiety, although it is true that many do lay msot of the blame for its formation on noxious social pressures, whether familial, corporate or national.[23] An increasing number of thinkers, however, are tracing this basic anxiety back further than the child's inability to cope with the vital-reactive demands of the earliest significant others. They would agree that the child does indeed adapt to these conflicting encounters with others from an early age by repressing his or her spontaneous self in favor of presenting a more acceptable, unspontaneous "idealized" self. They see also that these defensive reactive tendencies may indicate a response not only to human others but to an Otherness that goes beyond individual yearned-for maternal figures with whom one is always secure, or demanding paternal figures by whom one is called forth to perform well. The young child not only senses his powerlessness in the face of the world of powerful grown-ups and unfamiliar strangers who simultaneously attract him and make him anxious. He is also from the earliest moment a somewhat defensive openness to All That Is. This spiritual awareness is part of his relational dialogue with the persons, events and things that reality has to offer. When the defensive character structure of the client begins to emerge in the therapy session, the therapist who deals with it only in terms of psycho-social defense mechanisms and confines her perceptions of it to the closed circuit of the client's vital-personal reactions to past encounters with others, may miss entirely the "ontological" dimension of anxiety that may accompany this person's inability to connect with others in his world.

Distorting the meaning of the other

All anxious people (and everyone who is free is also to some extent anxious) tend to deal with other people in the only way open to an anxious person. We defend ourselves against unpredictable "otherness" by living out a somewhat defensive pattern of control and manipulation, of role playing and social pretension. Out of touch with our actual selves, we actualize only one rather narrow possibility in our relations with others. This patterned possibility will gradually emerge and can be picked up by a counselor either in our projections on others or in our illusions about ourselves, in the partial truths we cling to in our mistaken attachments. Because our defensive patterns are motivated by anxiety, they tend in the direction of reducing not only the world but the people in it to manageable size. That is, persons no longer emerge for us in the fullness of their reality as they are. Instead they are allowed to emerge either within the narrow confines of what the defensive ego perceived as controllable, or as substitute "little beyonds" whose magnified presence can serve as a defense against the even less controllable Greater Beyond that is at the origin of our most basic anxiety.

In view of this anxious two-fold possibility of distorting the meaning of the other, the therapist of a person who is having difficulties in his or her relatedness with others needs to have an understanding of several different mechanisms of distortion and illusion by which the client may be transferring not only former ways of relating onto a present situation, but also may be projecting onto another person the wished for ultimate meaning of his or her entire life.[24] In the first case, she will have to help the client to recognize what is unfree, infantile, fixated, narrow and unrealistic in his pattern of presence to other persons. In the second, the counselor may also have to help the client uncover his somewhat idolatrous substitution of another person for the ultimate horizon of Otherness. Actually, the exploration of either mode of distorted relatedness can become an exploration of the client's original anxiety, of his fear of moving beyond the familiar, of allowing otherness to emerge freely in uncontrolled unpredictable originality. Such an exploration, if it truly confronts the deepest homonomous desires within the human person, will inevitably move beyond the social or interpersonal into the realm of the transpersonal.

For now, I shall stay with the first mode as describing one aspect of what can happen between persons who encounter one another in a situation like therapy or spiritual direction. In such an encounter, whether between therapist and client, authority and subordinate, husband and wife, director and directee, teacher and student or friend and friend, two worlds of meaning come together and co-constitute a new world of meaning "between" the two persons. This new world between the two is further enriched by the horizon or ground out of which both parties emerge. However, when one of the persons is for some reason not free to allow the other to emerge openly for him in all his freedom and unpredictable complexity, this person, out of anxiety, fear or rigidity will tend to narrow his perception of the other. The other cannot, then, emerge in the true richness of the world of meaning he brings, but must be reduced and thereby controlled by the limited definition projected on him by the perceiver. This limiting definition projected on the other out of the perceiver's narrowed, rigid perception is called a transference.[25] A transference co-constitutes the other as an object, an object that is either more than its reality or less, depending on whether the perceiver needs to project ultimate desires for perfection and omnipotence (positive transference) or ultimate fears of evil and the demonic (negative transference). This, in brief, may be the phenomenon that accounts for some of the otherwise unexplained emotional overtones that accompany some therapeutic and/or spiritual direction sessions.

The perceiver may also co-constitute the other as controllable by allowing him or her to emerge in only one restricted level or aspect of their being. For example, a therapist or counselor may notice that some clients can only perceive others in their ability to function for them or in their ability to play a certain role, to give pleasure, or to supply admiration and protection. All other more challenging, dangerous or unexpected aspects of the other are effectively screened out by the selective perception of these clients. The other remains confined to the narrowness of the ego needs of these perceivers. There is little or no contact with the other as he or she *is* in reality, as a whole vital, personal, spiritual self, because these clients have confined their perception to one level of meaning. Although the vital and spiritual richness of the other is also present in the encounter, neither is allowed to emerge as figural for the repressed selves of those particular clients. In their anxious flight from spiritual openness, they have probably constricted their existence, and therefore their relatedness to others, to a mixture of the following three fairly typical coping patterns, with usually an emphasis on the style that makes them feel more secure.[26] It would be helpful perhaps if spiritual directors were as familiar as therapists seem to be with all three patterns.

Persons whose basic prepersonal tendencies are directed towards seeking to be one with or liked by others are most apt to seek out the fundamental meaning of their lives beyond themselves in the ideals and opinions of other people. Clinging to love, approval and acceptance that comes from outside themselves, they tend to project power and authority onto others and to live in the illusion that they themselves are thereby good, compliant, obedient inferiors. In their lifelong search for belonging and self preservation, they lose sight of their own wishes and desires. Their idealized self can become a tyrant, confining them to outwardly agreeable and charming, though inwardly worthless and inferior role playing. Unable to express anger or aggression, they are equally unable to be in touch with their own somewhat mean or power hungry side, and tend to be crushed when the other will not compromise and be agreeable. Basic anxiety attached to the inevitable experiences of human powerlessness prevents such people from seizing the initiative in human relations and narrows their relational possibilities to persons with whom they can feel safe, with whom they feel they belong, on whom they can lean and by whom they feel they will be protected, for example, a therapist or spiritual director.

Although apparently not self-seeking, such compliant persons are basically as horizontal in their mode of being as are the more aggressive types who appear to be their opposite. More outwardly active, the aggressive person seeks to be one with others not by begging for their approval but by taking initiatives in moving against them. Others are to be competed against and defeated, and are thus co-constituted as powerless victims of the "winner."[27] Converting anxiety over their own powerlessness into anger, the aggressive personalities have a narrowed perception of others mainly as useful for fulfilling their ego functional projects. Under their willful control, others become hostile objects to be defeated before their unpredictable hostility gets out of hand. The idealized self of such persons is a perfectionist who hardly ever allows them to relax or show tenderness to others. Usually out of touch with their weak, needy, compliant self, they despise those features in others also. Yet it is this very weakness in others that calls forth the generosity in such people, leads them to take responsibility for others, and to use their energy in active service for those weaker than themselves.

A third defensive style of reacting to the world of others arises from a basic pre-personal tendency directed away from what is other than the self in modes of withdrawal or avoidance. Detached persons choose to put a distance between themselves and the difficult or problematic others. Rather than attempting to placate or conquer other people, this type of person prefers the role of observer, outwardly calm and unaffected, inwardly free and uninvolved. Others are thus co-constituted as threats to one's privacy, to one's unimpeded freedom from coercion and restriction. Such a person must defend against the other who makes demands or clings, yet their own anxiety is always just below the surface in interpersonal relations, especially with others who threaten the appearance of serenity and wisdom they are striving to achieve. Such persons tend to preserve the illusion of the idealized self as non-competitive and serene by disowning their somewhat messy and limited actual self, and by staying out of involvement with as many of the concrete particulars of life as possible. They ask only to be left alone, yet if this actually happens the impoverishment of this lonely remoteness from others can become unbearable. At what might be called the opposite pole from the compliant personality type, the detached style of living tends to produce an independence from having to relate to others that can be both critical, non-possessive and in the long run, freeing for the other, who escapes idolizing projections and also perhaps the experiential warmth of human companionship.

Traces of all three of these styles are found in every dialogue with the world of others. Everyone lives with the anxiety of having been isolated and helpless in a hostile world, of not being able to cope, of needing to gain ego control over others. Everyone from time to time, to maintain the image of his or her ideal self, indulges in one or all of the above-mentioned illusions. This is the assumption underlying the current enthusiasm for transactional, gestalt and other group therapies that are centered on the dialogue we humans are with our world, and on the self-deceptive games we play in our relatedness with others as well as with ourselves. The crisis of identity that persons experience when self-imposed roles disappear is ample evidence of how trapped contemporary people are on the ego level of defensive interpersonal relations and societal illusions. Therapists and spiritual directors who are not trapped there themselves may be the only ones able to help people break through to a broader horizon than that of merely interpersonal relatedness as the basis for a fully human life.

CHAPTER VIII

THE PERSON FROM A SPIRITUAL POINT OF VIEW

Spirit in flesh

One way of approaching the struggle for freedom in the spiritual life is to see it as St. Paul does. Particularly in his letters to the Galatians and the Romans,[1] he recognizes people's experience of loss of freedom and the hope they have for its restoration. As one in touch with the mystery of faith, he sees their restricted lives not in terms of neurotic problems of relatedness or failure to achieve certain worldly goals, but rather he views their lack of freedom as bondage to the law, as a type of intentional relation to the world that closes them off from the Mystery of God and the fruits of life in the Spirit. It is this closed off intentionality that he refers to when he describes those who live according to the "flesh." Such persons have restricted their vision of reality to the external appearances of this world and find themselves embedded in sins of the body and divisiveness that may well end in mutual destruction. Real freedom would be to learn to live according to the "spirit" so that the intentionality of the whole person, body, soul and spirit, would be directed towards God, towards recreation in Christ, towards the redeeming invisible horizon that gives meaning to present sufferings and to the hope that animates the whole created world.

Paul also experiences the situated yet free human person as a transcending possibility of being restructured or changed. But he sees the destiny of that change as being not simply self-discovery and freedom *from* the old order of alienation and anxious interpersonal relatedness, but also as a freedom *for* the whole person to share in the glorious new order of being beloved children of God. In other words, the image of the human person out of which Paul sees freedom emerging is that of someone called forth in love to share a totally unmerited new life, the life of God himself. [2]

Moreover, according to Paul, it is the Spirit of him who raised Jesus from the dead and who dwells in the human person, who will accomplish this transformation from the old order to the new, from the life of the flesh to the life of the Spirit. The principle of this type of guidance is the Holy Spirit who witnesses to our true identity, who leads the children of God from their slavery to a realization of their divine destiny and who is the ultimate source of direction for those who seek to live a fully human spiritual life. Thus, the implicit assumptions and dynamics of the spiritual direction process differ considerably from those of therapeutic counseling; in fact, they may be directly the opposite at times. Paul indicates as much to the Galatians when he says: "Remember that you have been called to live in freedom — but not a freedom that gives free reign to the flesh . . . My point is, that you should live in accord with the spirit and you will not yield to the cravings of the flesh . . . the two are directly opposed. This is why you do not do what your will intends." [3] Here it is apparent that Paul's assumptions regarding the meaning of "freedom" and "will" are not at all the same as the meaning ascribed to these terms by contemporary psychology.

It is often difficult to detect this difference in view of the fact that the person who comes for spiritual direction does not appear at first glance to be very different from persons who present themselves for psychological counseling. Directees too could be described as basically healthy and desirous of enhancing their limited freedom, and as somewhat socially conditioned and defensive. To a certain extent past developmental history has probably alienated them from their true selves, locking them in a "character armor" and encapsulating them in somewhat fixated attachments to partial aspects of reality. Like persons who come for counseling, persons who seek spiritual direction will also usually be somewhat out of touch with themselves and for various reasons will have substituted a partially false self for the true self they actually are. They may also be experiencing a sense of conflict or restlessness at having been jolted into a more reflective stance by recent and unexpected events. They may be experiencing problems about self-identity, fixation on partial wholes, and/or encapsulation in ego and superego illusions. Very likely, as products of contemporary society, they will not have escaped at least some embeddedness in merely vital, personal, functional, social, scientific or aesthetic ideals. However, unlike their brothers and sisters who expect to work out their conflicts and problems regarding "freedom" and "will" within the context offered by that society, persons who come for spiritual direction sense that for them, the truth of their identity lies in a dimension of reality which somehow transcends the taken-for-granted meanings of the world view espoused by the majority of traditional psychologists and counselors; that for them, not only freedom and will, but also defensiveness, self-identity and encapsulation in partial wholes have different meanings because of the mysterious horizon against which they are seen in the Christian spiritual direction process.

As members of a culture that puts a high priority on one's capacity for interpersonal relatedness, people who seek spiritual direction are also likely to bring with them some of their confusion about seemingly conflicting desires for likeness and affinity with others and/or feelings of unlikeness and separation from others. However, un- like the psychological counselor, the spiritual director can- not ignore the "ontological" anxiety[4] that may underly this confusion, since she is more alert to the possibility that the person's original spiritual anxiety regarding the dimension of All That Is, is finally beginning to show itself. The task of the spiritual director, then, is not to deal with the directee's anxious defensive relational patterns as such but rather to point out how these lived patterns of perceiving other people may have been transferred to the present and either projected onto substitutes for the Abso- lute or have distorted the Absolute by positive or negative transferences. Thus, the director may focus on typical in- terpersonal relational patterns in spiritual direction not for the purpose of helping the directee get along better socially or even feel better about himself, but rather to show how these patterns tend to distort the directee's rela- tionship with God as well as with other people.

Similarly, preoccupation with the directee's tendency to create gratifying substitutes in place of the less than satisfactory realities that life hands him, may be picked up in a particular way by the spiritual director who sees that feeling good, safe or complacent must not be confused with spiritual living. It is at such points that the collision of the worlds of meaning of director and directee, the con- flict between the "flesh" and the "spirit," become more acute. We must look carefully not only at the contrast be- tween the "works of the flesh" and the "fruits of the spirit," but also at how the whole internal world of mean- ing of the person who comes to spiritual direction can be said to differ from the world of meaning that attracts a person to counseling, especially when the guidance or di- rection that is involved takes place in the horizon of Chris- tian revelation.

Called and free to respond

In a speech before the council of the Areopagus,[5] St. Paul points to the "already there" yet largely unknown God that human beings tend to worship as creator and controller of the cosmos. He tunes in to the Athenians' natural experience of the religious dimension of the universe, the invisible ground of their existence, and their recognition of it in their shrines to the unknown God. This unknown God is the existential context of all that the Athenians do and think and say. Paul knows that it is actually the Trinitarian God of Christian revelation in whom, did they but realize it, each one of them lives and moves and has his being. Further, this God is not far away but very near to them; he has raised his son from the dead so that each Athenian may find the way to living union with the mysterious presence he has merely sensed up until now in his life. Paul later claims that the destiny of each person lies in discovering his personal relationship with this mysterious horizon, because in the act of discovering God's presence in their lives, they discover who they themselves really are in the depths of their being. But scripture warns that this discovery cannot take place in relation to false gods made by human hands whose monuments substitute for the unpredictable God of mystery who was never made but simply *IS*. The whole of revelation points to this interpretation of what really is, and to the human person's destiny in relation to this reality, to God. It also indicates a brokeness in this living relationship between the whole person and his or her ultimate destiny, a falsification of both the human being and God, that prevents the fullness of what *is* from making its impact on fallible human life.

Persons who come for spiritual direction have, like the Athenians, already sensed or experienced in their own lives a touch of the "more than," a recognition that there is an invisible meaningfulness which they have just barely glimpsed beneath the visible factual appearances of everyday life. Perhaps these persons have experienced the spiritual dimension of all that is in some kind of unthematized religious experience, a moment of ecstatic openness to an initiative from the transcending horizon of mystery. More than likely such an honest moment of grace has been accompanied by a reflective glimpse of the actual unadorned self with its egoism and closedness; for the first time there is a dawning realization of the gap between our human world of appearances and transcendent reality. At such a moment, when the bottom seems to drop out of their formerly complacent world, thoughtful persons are inclined to seek help in exploring this new dimension of existence from another person, from someone who knows more about this unknown territory and is further along the path of union or participation in this reality than they are.[6]

Dissatisfaction with the formerly accepted horizontal modes of their divided culture may also impel such persons to seek out another way of being that complements the fresh vision of reality they have seen. No longer satisfied with a world of meaning that represses the spiritual dimension, men and women throughout the ages and in many different traditions and cultures have found themselves at some stage of their evolution seeking a more spiritual direction for their entire lives.

It is important to note that people are not awakened to the need for spiritual direction primarily by means of negative experiences, although some do find themselves confronting the spiritual dimension in the wake of jolting losses not unlike those described as motivating people to seek psychological counseling. But the majority of people who are interested in getting more in touch with deeper spiritual meanings are people who are apparently living fairly satisfactory lives already and are not in any severe sense out of touch with themselves or significant others. In view of a new possibility for growth in the "pneumatic" dimension of their being, their hearts are attracted to God and his will, to the search for peace, freedom, justice and life, to prayer and virtue, towards conversion or change to a deeper level of being than they have allowed themselves to experience so far.[7] To put it simply, they are drawn to God.

From the perspective of Christian revelation, the person who seeks spiritual direction has been created by God's love; is called forth to a destiny of intimate union with the Father in the Son through the Holy Spirit; and is capable of responding to or refusing this initiative of God's love towards him or her. Although the person is also called forth to relationship with others and with the universe of things and events in general, it is clear that for the baptized Christian all these relationships are somehow bound up with his or her relationship to God. Thus, any attempt to shift one's attention to the divine presence, to respond personally to God's initiative of love, that is, to pray or to live a prayerful life, will inevitably be bound up with and affect all these other relationships. False or unbalanced attitudes towards creatures will in turn affect prayer, in so far as they influence one's attitude towards God. In a word, primitive Christian anthropology sees each person's life as a whole, as an interpenetration of spirit and body, in which his or her spiritual or prayer life is always an incarnated life expressing itself in a body destined for resurrection. It is the "heart,"[8] that is the focus of spiritual direction, the pneumatized heart that is made for union with God but tends to stray far from that unity and lose itself in the false gods of sin and illusion, of truth-denial and ego-functional self salvation.

The person who comes for spiritual direction should be seen primarily as a man or woman capable of living a life of graced presence to God and as able to make personal choices in that direction, as a free subject of his or her own actions and decisions. Because human freedom is always a relative, limited freedom in need of being liberated from a multitude of false directions, this person may require help in bringing these capacities of knowing, loving and choosing into harmony with the deepest laws of the universe, so that all their "doing" finds its significance in the "being" context of their life of relationship with God. The point here is that the real limitations of the human condition must not make us lose sight of the fact that every human being is always also somewhat free to allow grace to penetrate and renew him, to respond to a vision of himself that goes beyond where he may find himself at any given moment.

Persons who have been baptized possess the beginning of this renewal and transformation, but at the center of the whole concept of Christian formation or self-direction lies each one's own personal and unique desire to choose to respond to that possibility of new creation. Without this focus on the freely choosing heart, Christian formation and spiritual direction retain the flavor of something that is imposed, that can be the result of skillful conditioning and well nigh irresistible educational techniques. To a greater degree than psychological counseling, spiritual formation and direction are dependent on the willing cooperation of the human person. A directee who does not choose to follow his or her own deepest directedness in response to the divine initiative will never reach the final goal of spiritual direction, which is awakening to the truth of what really is and surrendering trustfully to that Divine Other in all the relationships with reality in which his will is concealed.

It is important for the director to have some idea of how the person who comes for direction has completed the developmental tasks of human freedom up to this point in his or her life. The degree of ego strength, the sense of his own self-worth, an ability for spontaneous self-opening to the dialogical modes of being and a psychic capacity to love and will the good for others are all fundamental natural developments on which grace may build. So, too, is the balance of capacity for in-being and counter-being, for relationships of immanence and transcendence that guide the person's interpersonal encounters. A sense of solidarity with the human community, a sense of shared creatureliness, the recognition of finitude, and the need for salvation are also basic realizations on which the directee's personal relationship to the transcendent Other will depend.

Each periodic self[9] also brings with it certain limitations as well as fundamental possibilities for the growth of each individual man or woman who seeks to plunge more deeply into his or her self-transcendent direction. The lived virtues of faith, hope and love have their roots in and are facilitated by patterns of human growth and development[10] from earliest infancy through the stages of interpersonal and social relations to their final goal of surrender to the Eternal Mystery of love. The development of this triad points to the relation between natural psychological development and the spiritual life as a whole, and further exploration of this relation will contribute much towards an understanding of the human capacity for spiritual freedom.

Defensive and resisting

Having described persons who seek their spiritual directedness as being somewhat "awake" to the spiritual dimension, I must add immediately that these persons are also more or less spiritually "asleep." This sleep is a kind of torpor, a lack of awareness, a confusion about what is real in the self and in all that is not the self. It is a kind of blindness to what is there to be seen, a deafness to what is there to be heard. It is a state in which the person is closed off from truth, from reality, from what is. It is sometimes described in scripture as a hardness of the heart, a mode of relating that is not wholly open to the Mystery of all that is. In spite of the fact that they are made in the image of God and called forth to daily emergence by the divine initiative, persons who come for spiritual direction, like all human beings, always fall short of this calling; invariably they fail to measure up to the standard of dynamic wholeness; they find themselves always also in sin by the very fact of having been born. Again we sense the human difficulty not only in attaining the "spirit" self that we truly are, but even in waking up from our embeddedness in flesh to a real understanding of what that might entail. We are all familiar with the conflict, the unfreedom, experienced by every one of us regarding the possibility of becoming our true self and the actuality of daily living up to the demands of such a calling.

Here the theme of spiritual anxiety confronts us again as we ponder the inevitable concealment of one's true nature by the false self, of one's original uniqueness by a defensive "character armor," of the concealment of the nature of the Holy by manufactured idols. Like the person who comes for counseling, the man or woman seeking his or her unique spiritual path has no choice but to emerge as a contemporary consciousness, a psycho-social identity co-constituted by a divided, alienating culture. A product of twentieth century society that, in emphasizing ego-functional meanings, represses not only vital but also spiritual dimensions of reality, this person lacks the kind of freedom to which Paul refers. Necessarily cut off to a degree from a fulfilling wholeness of relationship to other persons, events and things, the average person in our culture has real difficulty in emerging[11] as a human being, to say nothing of the conflict he or she encounters when challenged to a newness of life by the Spirit of God. From birth every human being has been surrounded not only by misleading cultural assumptions about the nature of reality, but also by his or her own unique ways of defending against the anxiety-producing demands of All That Is. Caught in the tension between an anxious need to remain in the safety of familiar, sleepy immanence and an urgency propelled by their own spirit, to go beyond the already emerged self, most persons at one time or another experience a kind of spiritual crisis. The seldom verbalized life question becomes "shall I disregard the calls to self-transcendence and remain in the familiar embeddedness of the known, or shall I risk the unknown in a wholehearted involvement in unfamiliar situations, persons and ideals to which the attraction of God's spirit seems to be directing me?" To do the latter requires a grappling with the many obstacles and resistances to divine inspiration that have encapsulated and defended that person from the divine spirit for all the previous years of their life.

In biblical language, such a "spiritual revolution"[12] will require a discarding of the old self for the new, a gradual replacing of the heart of stone with a permeable heart of flesh, an abandonment of oxen, fields and, if necessary, even one's spouse in order to accept the invitation to the marriage feast. A more contemporary expression of the last requirement might be to describe it as waking up and responding to the call concealed in one's own spiritual directedness, which in turn will probably involve an abandonment of some false gods, idols or little beyonds that have served as a defense against the Great Beyond. It is clear that different people create different ways of closing themselves off from the invitation of the Spirit. One may have totalized possessions and embedded himself in a safe world of things, of status, skills and information, rules and regulations, amassed property and wealth — of all the good things one can "have" in this world. Another may be encapsulated in myriad possibilities of "doing," finding security in all kinds of good works, in socially relevant activities, in sports or aesthetic pursuits, in studies or in working on her own individual perfection. A third person finds salvation and safety in the world of interpersonal relations, in building up a circle of friends and loved ones or even contacts and acquaintances who give him the illusion of being someone special, of being necessary and depended upon by many other people. None of the above is wrong in and by itself, but only when it is absolutized by the person in a rigid, compulsive or hysterical fashion so that he is cut off from the true God by these idolatrous possibilities of "doing" and "having."[13]

The majority of persons in our culture who seek spiritual direction will more likely than not be caught in one or the other of those one-sided modes. Some spiritual writers prefer to describe the absolutizing of those idolatrous forms of doing and having as particular forms of sinfulness, and speak of the human person as caught in his or her own "predominant fault."[14] They point out that directees need to be awakened to the power of this form of sinfulness as an obstacle to God's self-communication. Other more or less sinful obstacles to relationship with God may take the form of "hidden life directors"[15] absorbed from early encounters with significant others and appearing as fixations in despair, guilt, self-rejection and compulsiveness; as repressed sexuality and aggression; or as a long standing inability to trust or appreciate the good in other people. Certainly in relation to other human beings, blind compliance combined with an inability to distance, or blind withdrawal combined with inability to trust the other are equally destructive of any kind of spiritual guidance, whether it be the one-to-one variety or in a larger group situation.

Guilt, both the neurotic and the social variety, may also play a large role in the directee's defensive stance,[16] especially if there is even partial awareness of how he has not been living up to the personal call of the Spirit in his heart. Confusion about the worth of his unique direction may also have led him to create an idealized self-image that contributes further to the alienation of his spiritual existence. The unconcealing and eventual abandonment of this and similar illusions, the letting go of partial wholes to which one has been defensively clinging, the putting aside of long cherished securities, can, and often does, constitute the most painful aspect of the spiritual direction process. Every person who seeks to move in the direction of a deeper spiritual life should do it with the awareness beforehand that some pruning of one-sided or sinful attitudes, some "letting go" of familiar habits and customs will be necessary before he or she can be liberated to fruitfully incarnate that deeper life in the world.

Sinful yet loved

From what has been said thus far about both the director and the person who comes for spiritual direction within the Christian tradition, a figure/ground structure has emerged.[17] Clearly, it is not possible to make sense of the phenomenon of specifically Christian spiritual guidance without referring to its ground or context, the content of Biblical faith in the triune God of Christian revelation. Actually it is this faith that responds to God as ultimate source of truth, goodness and salvation in Jesus Christ and through the Holy Spirit that is the center of all Christian spiritual guidance and direction. God in his loving initiative towards everything that is, must be the starting point for understanding this particular human encounter. God, not man, is the central factor in any exchange between persons that we would call spiritual direction or guidance. What is of primary importance is not what either the director or the directee does or feels or thinks. The focus is on who God is for them and on how they open themselves to his will as ultimate reality. It is discovery of, consent to, and cooperation with this will that gives dynamism to the process of Christian spiritual direction.

Without a conscious centering on the divine will or directedness "already there" in all of reality, the term spiritual "direction" would lose its precise meaning. The direction encounter is not an end in itself, but always points the participants in a "direction" beyond themselves, a direction that is at the same time shared yet unique for each one. Once this focus on what *is* above and beyond the merely individual self is understood, it becomes possible to see why the assumptions and dynamics of spiritual direction seem to be, and often are, opposed to those of counseling and psychotherapy. In therapeutic counseling, the human person and his interpersonal relations are the starting point. Spiritual direction, on the other hand, begins from the mystery of God's self-communication to all of creation; it is only in relation to this horizon of revealed meaning that the human person discovers the direction or meaning of his or her own existence, and that the process of spiritual direction makes sense.

Persons who seek spiritual direction in the Christian context are uniquely created images of God, with a determined biophysical, reactive, psychological, spiritual-human nature, and at the same time a baptized, graced possibility of relating intimately to this God in the likeness of a new creation in grace.[18] In appearance they are little different from candidates for psychological counseling, but there is within such persons an invisible "direction" waiting to unfold in relation to Mystery, in union with Christ who embodies the mystery in himself. In this sense it is possible to see the spiritual direction process as gaining its life and dynamism not from the interaction between director and directee but from participation in the larger life of God's love for the world.

Like the branch that lives only when it remains attached to and energized by the vine, so too the person who comes for spiritual direction only finds the life that he or she is seeking if the direction process itself is tuned in to the Source of direction for the whole universe, into the divine horizon of life, Jesus Christ. Thus, the person who seeks direction is assumed to be already sought by God, to be already a creation of his love and a possibility of going beyond the first creation to a new life of intimacy, to a second creation that in no way destroys but rather transforms the wholeness of what he or she already is.

Spiritual direction is not concerned only about the spiritual dimension of the person. It is concerned with the whole person, body, soul or psyche and spirit combined.[19] This wholeness, the "whole heart" in Biblical terminology,[20] which makes the person be most profoundly who he or she is, must be taken into account in spiritual direction. The human has its place too. The laws of human development and unfolding, of necessity and limitation must be respected and trusted as initially good and given by God. Spiritual direction that ignores the structures of human emergence and its implied limitations as well as its possibilities will not be helpful to real human beings who are called to respond to God's initiative in a truly human and whole manner.

However, and here we see the clearest difference between the counseling process and that of spiritual direction, there is according to spiritual thinkers, something unaccountably wrong with human persons. They somehow fall short of the glory of God, fail to measure up to the mark of dynamic wholeness, and find within their heart a deep disharmony between the self that is and the self that could be. Christians speak of this failure to measure up in which we find ourselves simply by having been born, as sin.[21] Sin is the basic inability to be who we most truly are, to become the self-transcendent response to God's love he is calling us to be. Sin, for the Christian, is what conceals true identity beneath a false life style; it turns human persons necessarily in on themselves and blinds them to true value. Sin that turns the heart away from its true destiny in God, is what has to be brought to awareness and dealt with in the process of spiritual direction.

Again, returning to the centrality of revelation, we find that in a Christian view of the universe all things, events and persons derive value from their relationship with God. Sinful tendencies direct our response to things, persons and events, our valuing of them, away from this relation.[22] One way that the sin of the person who seeks spiritual direction might be described would be to speak of it as valuing and desiring things, persons and events outside of their relation to God, in isolation from his creative will. So the persons who come are divided selves in this spiritual sense also. They have, in a variety of ways perhaps, broken or weakened this primordial relationship with God, and are engaged in the conflict between freely returning to a more profound relatedness or union (new self) or choosing to remain in the grip of the natural (or old) self that bestows its own valuing on false or substitute gods in isolation from what really is.

The tension or conflict, the central struggle in spiritual direction, is between "spirit" and "flesh" in the Pauline sense; between the values of God and our isolated evaluations; between his ways and our ways; between generous response to his will and isolated clinging to our own. Interestingly enough, the central conflict in the counseling situation is often identified as that between the actual self and the false or ideal self, that is, between two aspects of one divided human being. In spiritual direction, the person's dividedness is discovered to have been brought about by isolation from the true self that is to be found only in union with God.

It is not surprising, once the different structures emerge, that what appears as "finding one's life" in spiritual direction might appear as "losing" it in counseling, and vice versa. The dynamics of the one phenomenon, because of its unique aim and reality, may at times contradict the dynamics of the other. Christian directees, for instance, may from time to time appear to emerge less successfully and efficiently than persons who are "getting their heads together" via therapy. On the other hand, persons may emerge from counseling with their vital-reactive egos in perfect functional shape and be almost completely dead in the dimension of their spirit, because in and by itself, psychology can do nothing towards increasing the life of grace. However, spiritual directors can become respectfully aware of both necessity and possibility; psychological insight can uncover neurotic obstacles to freedom without necessarily narrowing the horizon of the client; and spiritual directors are able to consent to and cooperate with these dynamics that underlie God's work of redeeming and restoring the directee to union with the Trinity. It ought to be possible, without needlessly thwarting the dynamics of natural human emergence, for the person who comes to *either* situation to be transformed into a whole human being whose undivided heart is able to be given back freely to God to whom it eternally belongs.

In terms of inner dynamics the lives of persons who seek spiritual direction are rooted and grounded first of all in love of the Trinitarian God. Although originally created for contemplative presence to this mystery of divine indwelling, the average directees as a consequence of sin are somewhat blinded to this deepest truth of their being. Yet in the realm of the spirit there is no other path to knowledge of the self except through knowledge and love of God. So directees need to learn first of all how they are each uniquely "known and loved from without beginning in God's rightful intent."[23] Trusting faith in this mystery of God addressing them in Jesus Christ will be the basis for whatever personal decisions may have to be made as the direction of their call begins to unfold. Involvement with Christ often means risking to give up one's own way in order to move towards the future in the light of his direction.

Spiritual direction is essentially future oriented;[24] it aims to open the person to a new sense of life, to new motivations and dispositions, new projects and actions, all of which are perceived as valid for the directee in the light of his or her faith in the Paschal mystery of Christ's having been raised from the dead by the Father. The usual way that people come to an awareness of both God's love and his will for them, is through embarking on a life of contemplative prayer in keeping with their own unique capacity and calling and through learning to be adept at what has traditionally been known as "discernment" and more recently as appraisal or self-direction.[25] In view of the fact that both of these are major topics, I shall not treat them here. Instead we shall consider how it is possible to become lost in substitutions for God; in substitutions that, in their resemblance to the Real, can become one of the major problem areas in spiritual direction.

Lost in substitutions for God

Spiritual direction addresses itself primarily to persons' relationship to what really IS, to how they perceive the presence or absence of the Transcendent, to the false or illusory perceptions they may habitually project onto this transcendent horizon of life. The essence of this falsification of presence, which I call "pseudo-spirituality," lies in substituting other values, truths and illusions, other gods for the true God. Persons caught in pseudo-spirituality are resisting the fact that only God is God; they are projecting onto partial wholes the reverence due only to *the* Whole, and habitually engaging in a false perception of reality. Pseudo-spirituality consists in making a god out of something less than God, of transferring to limited objects feelings of wonder and love that belong only to God. Pseudo-spirituality could be compared to what the Old Testament prophets warned against as idolatry. They too saw it as a major obstacle to encounter, to an intimate relationship with the true God.

In order to facilitate the directees' encounter with the living God of revelation, the Christian spiritual direction process must include uncovering falsity and illusion;[26] helping the directees to take back some of the habitual projections and transferences that have distorted God's reality for them, to risk letting go of the false security those projections provide. It is understood by most directors that directees today usually bring with them distorted impressions of God from their childhood, culture, family or education, so that they will tend to perceive Him as a stern judge, an unrelenting punisher, a sentimental lover, an irrelevant cipher, and so on. At this point in time, we are aware of the many images of Christ that stir the minds of contemporaries: the Christ of popular piety; the Christ of the dogmatists; the Christ of political revolutionary action or inward peace and security; the Christ of the East and the Christ of the West; the Christ of literature; and the Christ of the various theologies both within and outside the Church.[27]

But the problem goes much deeper than simply an erroneous impression of God or Christ that can be corrected by means of proper instruction. Illusory perceptions of God stem not only from the intellect, but also from the will. Human persons in their willful need to feel autonomous and self-sufficient, basically do not desire to see God as he is, or to recognize that he is the absolutely necessary lifegiving ground of whatever figural life style they are engaged in. In anxious attempts to deny the absolute power of the Lord of the universe (the Absolute Other), human beings have always been inclined to create smaller, more manageable universes of meaning, that can provide them with a substitute for the original openness to the Sacred into which they have been born.

One manageable "little beyond"[28] in which humans tend to feel safe and secure is the domain of cultural religion, of what Freud and others after him have deemed "religious illusion," a mere projection of the infantile need for security. Unfortunately Freud was not altogether mistaken. Many people, even those who seek spiritual direction, may unconsciously be caught in a spiritless religion[29] that, while denying their openness to All That Is, serves to defend them from the anxiety of confronting the God of mystery, the God who will not fit into our human need for control and predictability. This transcendent God, who is the focus and context of Christian spiritual direction, has revealed himself also as an immanent and loving God. Nevertheless, as Absolutely Other, he is totally beyond human prediction and control. Such an unknown God might truly constitute a threat to human security, but in Christ he has revealed his merciful love and comes incredibly near to man. The creatures of this God are also always free to reject the risk of his nearness, to distort the original desire they are for union with this mysterious Other, and to lock themselves into the illusory sleep of what some philosophers call the "natural attitude."[30] This possibility of falsifying one's relationship to God as Other, as truly God, to avoid the tension and anxiety that accompanies the exercise of freedom, must be unconcealed and dealt with in the spiritual direction process.

As in counseling, the issue is one of human freedom. Persons who come for spiritual direction are really free to deny God as God, to isolate themselves in an absolutized man-made religion of manageable observances, of compulsively obeyed do's and don'ts, of socially constituted cultural organization that guarantees salvation in a marketing economy exchange for rigid practices and adherence to a more or less materialistic religious security system. Marx and others have pointed out this contradiction of religion as a social product, as a kind of escapist "opium" that lulls into sleep the anxiety that might otherwise seize persons in confrontation with the living God. But even if human beings are not caught in this particular "spiritual materialism,"[31] there are many other ways in which they can alienate themselves from real contact with God.

Each human person is naturally a longing for ultimate Being, but in daily life we encounter only concrete limited beings. There is an almost unavoidable tendency to transfer or project onto these limited beings the feelings of expectant adoration that are appropriate only to the Ultimate Other, to God. So parents, teachers, friends, marriage partners, bosses, even institutions or one's country become objects of our "positive religious transference." As illusory objects of absolutized worship, they become, in fact, idols of worship, so glorified that they are no longer experienced as the limited realities they really are. Sooner or later, however, it will become evident to the worshippers that these idolized objects do not live up to their expectations and that they cannot be completely satisfying. They are then demoted from god to demon and become the despised object of our "negative religious transference." The disappointed persons may then close off from these concrete daily realities and withdraw to a more ideal "spiritual" world out of touch with concrete people and things. In either case, whether of illusion or disillusion, directees tend to lose touch with the living and true God.

In the first case, it is clear that a partial whole, a person, event or thing, is substituted for the Whole itself. The person may be totally fixated on certain limited but fascinating persons, practices or even religious institutions and may mistake them for the whole of reality, instead of recognizing their participation in the mystery that still lies beyond them. The spiritual director must also be prepared to cope with the negation when it occurs; when a young person comes up against the human imperfections of certain members of his community or the community of the Church itself and begins to think of giving up on Christianity; when a newly married woman discovers that her husband is not perfect and begins to think her decision to marry was a mistake; when another directee discovers that her life so far has been largely inauthentic and becomes discouraged to the point of self-hatred. The director must help the counselees to accept the fact that the people, events and things of their daily life, while limited, are still the most radical source of contact with God. In cutting themselves off from them in favor of a more "spiritual" life, they are cutting themselves off from the Holy, who is their Source.

On the other hand, there is much to recommend the healthy experience of negative transference or the withdrawal of projections, since directees may then begin to recognize that their untimate desire is for God alone, a desire that will not be completely or permanently satisfied by any of its limited manifestations. Directees may gradually come to accept the limited goodness of the persons and events of life; at the same time they may realize the need to move beyond them without having to either idealize or negate themselves or the persons and events. Without benefit of infantile illusions, they can simply see and experience things, people and events as they are in their reality, as manifestations of, but never substitutes for, their Creator. They can love them because they have first loved and accepted themselves and God.

A profound connection exists between a person's relations with people and his or her relation with God; the spiritual direction process is thus concerned with the directees' natural attitudes towards others — their vital-reactive tendencies towards jealousy, envy, lust, desire for power and control, possession, dependency, etc. Again, both positive and negative possibilities come into play as the directees tend to perceive others as all good or as all bad; in this illusion they resist their otherness by living in a positive compliant project of "being nice," or a more negative project of being aggressive or antagonistic, or simply of withdrawing from the other.[32] The stripping of illusion that accompanies learning to let the other be all that he or she is, without imposing expectations, magic claims or manipulative controls, can be extremely helpful in reorienting the directee's attitude towards God.

Highly anxious about "otherness" in general, the overly compliant directee will tend to cut down the fearful risk by reducing God to a powerful and safe protector or hiding place, or even to an approving mother figure before whom he or she can act the role of a yes-saying "plaster saint," who keeps all the rules and is never able to admit to any angry feelings or sinful inclinations. Such persons, in their desire to please, may tend uncritically to take over the idolatrous gods that the culture has fashioned for them. Yet for all their weakness, they are the most ready to accept and to trust in God's initiatives of merciful love in their regard.

The more actively agressive directee, because he or she is accustomed to seizing the initiative, is more likely to worship uncritically the idols built by their own hands. Proudly taking control of their lives, such persons are also anxious about their powerlessness before the Holy, and may tend to "use" God as a function of their own self-salvific projects. However, these same persons are also likely to respond with energy to the divine "call" of revelation and spend themselves tirelessly in building a better world.

It is the third type, the detached, who will probably not build idols themselves nor uncritically take over those of others. Less likely to be trapped in concrete embeddedness, they may also miss the message of revelation simply because it is involved in the concrete particulars of the world. It is hard for such persons to admit their need for a savior or to commit themselves with any permanency, but in the long run they are also most likely, without possessiveness or forcing, to allow God to be God, to be "Other" than their own projections would have him be. In any case, the "purgative way" for the person who really desires transformation or conversion of heart will begin here, with whatever vital reactive tendencies characterize his or her "natural attitude," and with the willingness to expose and deal with them in the process of spiritual direction.

Saved by the Spirit

That there are obstacles to the life of grace in each of us and in our culture is evident. Born into a basic human predicament that includes a strong though often unconscious resistance to truths that seem to threaten feelings of personal importance and security, most men and women build natural defenses against letting God be God in their lives.[33] Unconsciously anxious and mistrusting the call of the transcendent, they find it more possible and logical to trust the evidence of their senses, to seek security in technological evolution or socio-political revolution, or simply to extend the horizontal modes of interpersonal relationship rather than to place their trust in an ambiguous highly challengeable God. Directees are looking for answers to the question they are, and this world offers them a multitude of philosophies and world views. In directs spiritual seekers to the youth culture, to romanticized third and fourth worlds, to psychoanalysis and Eastern meditation, to cybernetics and socio-behavioral utopias. It presents them with a horizontal context for all of life in terms of interpretations based on interpersonal or even transpersonal ideologies. All of these apparently worthwhile endeavors can and do become obstacles to the life of grace when totalized within a too narrow perspective. Yet the contemporary person who comes for spiritual direction will usually be somewhat trapped in at least one aspect of the pervading social anxiety, in the illusion of having to become a "personality," or in the compulsive need to be somebody. Problems of inauthentic selfhood, of the repression or denial of one's deepest subjectivity in favor of the self as an improvable, controllable object, bring about a disruption in the person's relation to self and others. Also, in their tendency to encourage self absorption, they can separate him from relation to what transcends the self.

It is only as persons grow gradually in conscious awareness of and relation to Transcendent Reality, that they can become detached from the persons, places, things, ideologies and manifold "little beyonds" to which they have been clinging for safety and security. The way to freedom lies in nonattachment, not only to merely horizontal or ego modes and values, but also to the social pretences behind which we hide the limited mixture of acceptable and unacceptable factors that we actually are.

"Becoming who you are" really does describe one of

the major tasks of the spiritual direction process. It is a task that cannot be carried out unless there is a growing realization of the truth that it is in Christ that we are; it is in him alone that we truly "live and move and have our being."[34] The person who comes for direction needs first of all to get in touch with this reality. Then he or she will be able to face the misdirected, unreal, illusory modes of thinking and being that have unconsciously dominated all their relationships up until now, especially their relationship with God.

This above-mentioned purification of isolating anxious ways of being and behaving, whether in relation to self, others or the Ultimate Other, will be accomplished in spiritual direction by the Holy Spirit. The spiritual director must humble admit his or her powerlessness before the alienating reality of human sin, guilt and anxiety. Just as the mass of Christians can get lost in the taken for grantedness of familiar "church" formulas and institutions, so the individual directee can and will lose himself in complacent but empty rituals of religion unless the Spirit breaks through with unpredictable new meanings and a new heart. Allowing God to be God, allowing things and people to emerge as they are from a loving and compassionate Divinity, allowing oneself to be vulnerable to a will that is not of one's own choosing, and bringing forth "fruits of the spirit"[35] is impossible without trust that can survive moments of doubt, darkness and seeming separation. It is a trusting attitude, one that risks saying "yes" in spite of tension, doubt and guilt that will eventually open the directee up to the loving presence of the Holy at the heart of existence. This trust impells him to move on in the direction of the illuminative pull of the God who draws him. Here we touch again the deep conflict that underlies Christian conversion. In spiritual living directees must eventually risk turning to a freedom based no longer on pious feelings, social approval or the relative alienation of any cultural substitutes, but rather on direct dependence on an invisible, inscrutible Other who is also always free. At the same time they are upheld by gratuitous gifts of grace that build on and transform the already present natural human attitudes of faith, hope and love so that their original anxious perception of what seems to be may be transformed into a more confident, surrendered discovery of what really IS.

CHAPTER IX

THE PRESENCE OF THE THERAPIST

Influential personal presence

We turn again to the world of psychotherapy and to an examination of some developments regarding the therapist's role that may prove enlightening to anyone called to be a spiritual director or guide. The quality of the guide's presence and its importance for the outcome of the encounter is one notion that connects these two roles. I am reminded of a traditional Chinese legend that tells of a remote village where a long drought had dried up the fields to such an extent that the harvest was in danger of being lost and the people were facing starvation. The villagers did everything they could. They prayed to the ancestors; they paraded around the fields with the priests carrying images from the temples; they set off fire crackers and made offerings. But their rituals and prayers failed to bring the rain. In desperation they sent far away for a man reputed to be a "rainmaker." When the old man arrived, they asked him what he needed in order to do his magic. He answered that all he needed was a quiet place where he could be alone. So they gave him a little house, and he lived there quietly doing the ordinary things everyone does in life, and on the third day it rained.

People commenting on this legend[1] are quick to point out the qualities of the old rainmaker's personal presence as illustrated in the legend. He did nothing extraordinary. He simply went about his daily business without fuss, without doing anything special or giving a lot of advice. He did not even consciously "help" anyone else. He was in fact hardly noticeable at all, yet around him, in his presence, good things began to happen. The rain came and gradually the fields sprouted, blossomed and bore fruit; the people were nourished and the whole environment changed in a positive way. The old man was simply being who he was, neither causing nor preventing the rain but simply allowing it to fall. His receptive allowing presence affected those around him more powerfully than any direct effort of his will could have done. In spite of the fact that he did not use power to make anything happen, his very presence allowed life in all its fullness to burst forth around him. For them he was, as one writer puts it, a "beneficial presence."[2]

In this chapter I shall look particularly at the guide, therapist or counselor as a beneficial or at least influential presence in her relation to the other or group of others. Much of value has been written about what the helping person should or should not do. I am interested here in exploring how the helper, by her very way of being, by the quality of her presence, even more than by her activity or doing, influences the other who comes to her. If the structure of the guidance situation can be described as a coming together in space and time of two or more persons who are reflectively present to each other in a more or less influential way, then it is important to understand something of how at least one of them, the counselor, can be said to "co-constitute" the other, in some way to "make the other be" or "call the other forth." It is, after all, the counselor's unique personal perspective on reality, her relatively open or closed, broad or narrow, rigid or flexible perception of persons, events and things that is the origin of her effective presence to the other. The counselor's vision of reality defines not only her approach to all its aspects, but also her ability to be a beneficial presence to persons who may seek her help. This chapter will deal mainly with an exploration of some of the ways in which a guide's perspectives on reality and her inner attitudes towards it condition how she spontaneously reacts and even consciously acts towards the world of others.

Like the old man in the legend, a disinterested, non-egoistic counselor's presence may "allow the rain to fall" and as a result her clients may grow and blossom forth. On the other hand, the insecure counselor who is driven to achieve a cure by manipulative "doing," may actually prevent life and growth from happening around her by the very nature of her controlling presence. Moreover, no counselor's presence is completely neutral. Contemporary psychological theory is making us increasingly aware of the fact that what happens in the counseling or guidance situation is never determined solely by the "problems" of the person who comes. Prereflective inner attitudes, basic predispositions, and implicit or explicit assumptions about the nature of reality, the nature of the human condition, the way things naturally are, color the perception of all counselors without exception. It is by examining some of these implicit contemporary images of the human person uncovered by psychologists themselves that we shall begin our discussion of the possible influence of the counselor's personal presence on what may or may not happen in the guidance situation.

Unacknowledged perceptual limitations

Perhaps the most powerful determiners of human thought and action, are the unconscious assumptions every person has about what it means to be a human being. Seldom raised to an explicit level of consciousness, these implicit assumptions, rooted as they are in life and experience, carry a prereflective charge that influences the decisions and choices of individuals and groups on a primordial level. One area of particular interest to counselors and therapists where these prereflective assumptions have been operative is in the realm of humanity's perennial quest for liberation from its bondage to the limitations of the human condition in the face of the universal desire for transcendence, for freedom, for "more than" what immediate reality has to offer. As long as there have been human beings, there has been the experience of unfreedom, alienation, captivity and lack of ability to go beyond impediments to freedom. What is most fascinating is that within each generation, and often among the individuals of each generation, there is always a wide variety of concepts about the nature of the impediments, and also about the nature of freedom itself and the process of liberation required to attain it.

In our twentieth century Western civilization, if people were asked to be explicit about the sources of human unfreedom, some would unhesitatingly speak in terms of exploitive socio-economic, racist and sexist structures embedded in the society itself. Others would mention the conditioning that results from our having to live in various misguided contemporary thought patterns derived from social classes, ethnic groups, religious beliefs and other sociocultural sources. Still others would see our unfreedom in terms of the vulnerability, frailty and limitations of the human body, or in the lack of knowledge and skill to overcome the impediments to human liberation that still plague the human mind. There are those who would not distinguish the sources of unfreedom even this explicitly, but would still tend in their actions towards either an optimistic or a pessimistic view of the steps we are able to take on the road to freedom.[3] One fact is evident: all human persons, whether they recognize and make it explicit, or leave it unexamined in their preconscious depths, are influenced in their encounters with the world and others by an image of the human person that partially co-constitutes the quality of their presence to reality.

Whether the counselor or therapist is mainly guided by a prereflective perception of powerful forces of domination in the society or by a sense of the inevitable powerlessness of man's vulnerable psychic self, will make a great deal of difference to the process of liberation she chooses on the conscious level. Whether this process is accompanied by optimism regarding man's ability to cooperate in his own liberation, or pessimism in the face of his nature as the determined outcome of conditioning by forces beyond his control, will also affect the way the helping person goes about this task. Even religious gurus and best friends are not immune to the prereflective influence of their image of the human person, though they may be even more likely to deny its existence or to assume that everyone sees the other as they do.

It is possible for someone in a position of guidance to acknowledge adherence to one or the other contemporary scientific "model" of social effectiveness based on an implicit image of the human person, without ever having actually made its underlying assumptions about reality explicit and without understanding how these unacknowledged assumptions affect the aims and goals of the counseling endeavor. For example, when faced with the task of helping a group to move beyond the narrow scope of their immediate limited condition in society, an idealistic teacher whose view of reality inclines her to see all others as products primarily of their socio-cultural environment, will probably aim to liberate them by helping them change what they believe about reality, and thus transcend their socio-cultural environment and attain liberation from cultural conditioning. Another consultant, who sees the human person's freedom as being obstructed by economic structures, is going to encourage that same group towards concrete revolutionary action, rather than attempt merely to alter beliefs about the nature of reality. Under the aegis of the biological model, with its underlying assumptions about man's genetic inheritance from a long line of predecessors, an ethologist given the same task might instead concentrate on helping the group towards liberation by encouraging them to live more comfortably with their own "animality." A therapist dealing with the same people, who happens to adhere to the behavioristic model, might opt for liberation from bad habits of behavior learned through faulty conditioning from the environment via certain techniques of behavior modification. An Eastern guru might demonstrate how by means of some form of ecstatic experience, the minds of his audience could be set free from the coldly logical prison of Western rationalism in which their society has trapped them.

In all these models, it is clear that an image of the human person as more or less determined by the environment, by cultural, socio-economic, genetic, behavioral and rationalistic forces beyond his or her control predominates. Yet it is doubtful whether the teachers, consultants, and therapists, in fact, the majority of persons whose actions and encounters within the human community are governed by these model, have ever consciously attempted to explicate clearly for themselves the more or less positivistic, deterministic nature of their underlying assumptions about human nature. It is even more probable that most parents, lawmakers, politicians, and custodians of public mores have never acknowledged the more or less deterministic nature of the limitations that continue to narrow and rigidify their perception and actions on behalf of those for whom they are responsible.

Limitations of psychotherapeutic presence

Counselors and therapists, as already indicated, are not immune to modification of their perceptual presence to the other by contemporary models of psychological effectiveness similar to those that guide the actions of the movers and changers of society. The counselor's presence as modified by an implicit image of the human person provides the ground for perception of the other in a counseling session. This fact gives heightened importance to his or her choice of therapeutic model. According to whether he or she acknowledges adherence to the psychoanalytic, behavioristic, interpersonal, existential, social cultural, humanistic or interdisciplinary model, the psychological counselor will view problematics and listen according to an often unacknowledged underlying orientation. Let me give a few intentionally oversimplistic examples to illustrate this point.

Because they see the other as determined by instinctual biological drives and unconscious desires and motivations, psychiatrists who adhere to the Freudian model, approach the human person with the aim of getting to the origin of defense mechanisms and the repetitive core of infantile fixations and repressed impulses that have developed as a result of past encounters. They listen for and encourage the patient to talk about past experiences in the context of a strong transferential attachment to the therapist. Jungian, Adlerian, or even Rogerian therapists, because their model of therapy assumes a different image of the human person, would look not only for different problematics in the patient's developmental history but would listen to his whole life story in a different way — the Jungians perhaps attuned to the collective unconscious and mythic, symbolic universals of the patient; the Rogerians attuned more to his underlying organismic feeling life.[4] In fact, Freudian patients eventually seem to even produce dreams with Freudian (sexual and aggressive) content, while Jungian patients bring symbolic dreams of archetypes and mandalas. Is this because just as what we look for is what we see, so what we listen for is what we hear? It is important for anyone involved in a counseling situation to realize that the way one listens, what one looks for, probably emerges from that available model of therapeutic presence which most nearly coincides with one's underlying orientation, the perceptive consciousness that one is. Perhaps it would be wise for counselors to be more conscious of the underlying image of man they personally hold, since it is the ground for their being together with the other in the therapeutic situation. The director's implicit image of the human person also provides a ground for the person who comes to the spiritual direction situation.

Contemporary thinkers are not limited to psychoanalytic models in relating to those in need of guidance. With the development in the twentieth century of the sciences of sociology and anthropology, the emphasis of the psychological models shifted to the image of the human person as a social being. This focus on the ongoing social processes that surround us in the larger socio-cultural milieu as well as in the immediate web of interpersonal and familial relationships in which personality develops, resulted in increased attention to the present here and now situation as also providing material for the therapeutic exchange. Psychologists and counselors in these models are likely to see the patient's maladjustment in terms of how badly he or she communicates and interacts with other people. They listen for defense mechanisms that have been adopted to shield the patient from threatening interpersonal relations or to support invalid societal roles. They are alert for the defensive games people play and for sickness in the form of faulty family patterns and isolation from lack of human communication in both the past and the present.

Therapists adhering to the sociocultural model like Adler, Horney, Sullivan and Fromm, Berne and Laing bring out the relationship between socio-cultural conditions and mental disorders, between the particular stresses to be found in Western society and the breakdown of the individual persons who comprise it. Pointing as they do to the prevalence in our society of the will to power and competition, of active versus contemplative values, of materialism and consumerism, of work orientation versus leisure and relaxation, of functional control as the favored mode of being, they have brought out the negative as well as the positive aspects of our being with others in the world. No counselor or teacher, therapist or guru, can afford to ignore the web of relationships that constitutes the client, student or disciple. The findings of these theorists may also indicate that while an image of the human person as "also always social" is essential, in and by itself it is not adequate to approach fully the reality of the human condition. Nor are techniques of social coping, such as sensitivity training, transactional analysis, confrontation groups and all the other manifold means of creative learning employed by a skillful, socially adept counselor, sufficient to meet the needs of all troubled persons who come seeking help. Here again, there may be a real limitation in the presence-as-ground of a therapist whose implicit image of the human person remains embedded in the merely social dimension of existence. Even more evident is the limitation of a spiritual director whose view of the human person is confined to the narrowness of the social relational problems that inevitably accompany spiritual search.

Although some of the above mentioned models embody a more or less negative idea of the human person as "problem" whose causes must be determined and dealt with, there are other models that embody a more positive view of the human person as "possibility," that is, as also always somewhat free to take a stand within his or her limitations. Some have already been mentioned. Others are to be located within what is called the humanistic or existential schools, in the so-called Third Force and transpersonal movements involving people like Maslow, May, Rogers and Perls. In this more optimistic view, the human person is seen not merely as capable of moving from maladjustment to adjustment but as being essentially on the way towards personal growth and as primarily needing to find a socially constructive and personally meaningful life style in order to fulfill his or her potential. In this model, one finds more emphasis on the future, on terms like love, creativity, values, meaning, personal growth and self fulfillment as well as on interpersonal and socio-cultural progress. The counselor who adheres to this orientation tends to look upon faulty social learning and exaggerated defense mechanisms not so much as indicative of abnormality or pathology, but as constituting blocks to potential growth, as obstacles that get in the way of the person's fulfillment. Thus, the Human Potential Movement's underlying image of the human person stresses basic health and freedom rather than the socially conditioned and defensive aspects of existence.

A balance for this optimistic view of the human being as unique, valuing and free is found in the existential model's emphasis on the situated aspects of that freedom — on the irrational, confusing, changing, sometimes absurd aspects of the contemporary social predicament. With its stress on man's freedom of choice and personal responsibility to embody socially constructive values, models in this approach encourage the counselor to place more and more of the responsibility for the outcome of the therapeutic encounter on the clients themselves. They are seen as subjects of their own actions rather than as objects to be manipulated or controlled or even helped by her. Relying less on the scientific skill of the counselor and more on the client's inner capacity for self definition and deciding what are for him meaningful links with the world of persons, events and things, this approach may well be more appropriate for clients who are nonpsychotic and able to be open to the added anxiety such risk involves.

The point I wish to emphasize here is that even in the case of working with a psychotic person, the therapist or counselor will be motivated either by an implicit image of the human person that denies the reality of even marginal freedom and responsibility, or she will respect, count on and never lose sight of that spark of free choice that is the core of every human being — the evokable dignity that sets us apart from the rest of created reality. Not only counselors and therapists, but social workers, medical personnel, parents, religious leaders, advisors and "carers" of all kinds, live their daily practice out of some prereflective image of the human person that governs not only their perception of the other but also what, if any, free response is evoked in him by whatever limited presence this prereflective image allows them to bring to the counseling or guidance situation.

Ways of evoking the other

There should be then no possibility for the counselor or therapist to live in the illusion of being simply a neutral technician, applying skillfully worked out theories and techniques to the somewhat passive objects of their concern. The counselor's presence, the orientations she actually lives towards all aspects of reality, is the real therapeutic instrument. I counsel others, not from a set of techniques, but from the actual person that I am. A false, distorted, or limited image of the human person will, in the dialogue between counselor and client, co-constitute and evoke the other in a false, distorted and limiting way. Instead of being a helpful beneficial presence, the counselor living in a narrow closed horizon of meaning, if often a reductive, reifying and unfreeing obstacle to the other's growth and self-emergence. Even the person's problems can be distorted by the narrowness of the counselor's horizon, by her inadequate reflection on the implicit philosophy or anthropology that underlies her basic image of the human person. The ground or horizon in which the counselor dwells and out of which she perceives, includes a thoughtful view of human freedom as well as of its determinisms and limiting factors. It implies also an explicitation of the significance of the world and human society, of ultimate destiny and the obstacles that prevent us from attaining that destiny.

In order to evoke the human person in his wholeness, the counselor's image must include an appreciation of vital reactive modes of presence (those that stem from bodily needs, drives, feelings, passions and impulses); of conscious rational controlling modes (those that stem from involvement in individual, social, aesthetic and functional possibilities); and of what one personality theorist calls preconscious and supraconscious dimensions of human presence as well.[5] Such an appreciation of the whole range of modes of presence will prevent totalization of any one mode, the instinctive over the aesthetic for example, or the ego-functional over the social and/or spiritual. It will also prevent totalization of a helping technique (such as Freudian interpretation, behavior modification, dream analysis, or confrontation), and will allow both persons to be open to the dimension of the spiritual as it exists in the totality of reality and as it evokes a response in the human heart. Without such an appreciation, it is as difficult for the counselor, as it is for anyone else who personally prefers one particular mode of presence, to avoid evoking that mode in the client.

To return for a moment to the Chinese legend mentioned at the beginning of this chapter, we find that the presence of a person who is primarily affirming and receptive, evokes life and growth in others. If, instead of allowing the other to be, the counselor insists on actively trying to exert influence or to have power on a horizontal level, the other will probably be evoked in equally horizontal modes of aggressive resistance, frightened withdrawal or false compliance, Moreover, the listening attitudes and therapeutic aims of a counselor who lives out of a broad horizon of values that is open to spiritual meanings will be modified by this horizon.[6] At the same time, within this broader horizon that includes a variety of values, she will be able to integrate the findings of the other models which embody important truths about partial aspects of the client's existence.[7] This broader horizon of the therapist's values may also be evocative of new ways of being and doing for the client, whose capacity for going beyond or transcending his present self is challenged in the relationship with another who offers alternative ways of being present in the world.

The counselor or therapist who embodies a holistic image of human possibility can become a "beneficial presence" for the other,[8] a "rainmaker" who influences not through what she can *do,* but rather by means of actually *being* a channel of spiritual values, a conscious spiritual perspective on life for the sake of the other's growth. As beneficial presence, the counselor is interested not only in the "problem," in what is *wrong* with the client, in maladjusted avoidance behaviors and their causes, in pathological symptoms and their removal. The counselor is also consciously interested in the positive potential for unfolding in freedom, wholeness, love, honesty, gratitude and peace — in the "mystery" that lies in every human person. Perceiving others as also cherishing certain spiritual values, which may or may not always be positive and health-promoting, the counselor is more alert to the powerful effects of these values on these person's relationships not only to the persons, events and things of their world, but also on what they set up as being of ultimate value, as being "god" in their lives. As a beneficial presence, the counselor or therapist will not allow manipulation of the client's positive or negative transference relationship with her to become the major focus of the therapy because she recognizes a horizon of valuing that goes beyond any interpersonal relationship — the horizon of ultimate spiritual meaning. As a dweller in this value context herself, she prefers allowing the client's life to unfold in relation to this larger horizon rather than be narrowed to the context of the transference love that is the usual accompaniment of most merely interpersonally oriented therapeutic relationships.[9]

Need for self-knowledge

The need of all counselors for self-knowledge, for self-awareness, for discovery of their own real life as response before helping others to do this, becomes more and more evident. They must attempt to discover the invisible positive contextualization they bring by way of benevolent intentions, by an integrative image of the human person, and by a certain well thought out hierarchy of values; they must also begin to acknowledge the negative aspects of their presence to the other. In order to avoid the "fiction of nondirectiveness,"[10] counselors must see themselves not only as value-bearers who are good for the other, but also as value-concealers whose own needs and distortions of reality may have a negative effect on the free unfolding of the client or group of persons they are supposed to be helping. I have already alluded to the fact that the object of the counselor's interested presence — what tends to catch his or her attention in the ongoing flow of experiencing the other — is what is most likely to become figural for both in the therapy situation. If the counselor's awareness is attuned not to positive values but rather to her own inner need for admiration, affection and being needed, or to her desire to control and influence others, to exert power or impose values on them; if the counselor's attention to the other is motivated by unacknowledged sexual fears and tensions or by the need to dominate and appear clever; if she actually harbors a despairing, negative image of the human person or is unable to tune in to her own countertransferential reactions[11] of panic, over-involvement, compliance and/or aggression, or over identification; if the counselor is unable to flow with the other's need to probe the spiritual dimensions of existence and becomes defensive whenever anything of this nature appears in their discussion — then it is safe to guess that she needs to deal honestly and acceptingly with some of these personal problematics before she will be free and disinterested enough to become a fruitful presence in the life of anyone else.

It is this need for personal liberation from their own limitations that sooner or later leads the majority of counselors and therapists to become clients and patients themselves, if only temporarily. The therapist, teacher or guru, the consultor or best friend who has little or no awareness of his or her own emotional experience or who is distracted from paying attention to the other by the loudness and insistence of his or her own strong feelings for or against the other, is a less effective instrument than one who is able simply to let go of self-absorption and allow the other to tell his story. The fewer unresolved conflicts there are in the counselor, the fewer opportunities the counselee is offered for avoiding his own freedom and responsibility, and the more likely it is that the latter will benefit from being in the healing presence of the counselor, who has already told her story to someone else.

People in the position of guiding and counseling others need to be aware of their personal need for liberation from their own vital-reactive tendencies and the narrowness of their reductive ego-horizon. They must recognize that they are not simply a well-intentioned and neutral listener, a sort of anonymous sounding board, nor are they merely an all-knowing interpreter or analyst of the objectified other. They are fellow humans whose own lived style or sense of life is underlaid by an implicit view of reality that probably needs to be liberated from certain personal and cultural limitations. In speaking mainly of personal limitations, I may appear to have neglected the less obvious but no less constricting socio-cultural assumptions that may be hampering the counselor's approach to the wholeness of the client's welfare. I refer to those pervasive attitudes that define successful living in terms of competitiveness and the drive for ego-enhancement, or in terms of vitalism and the over-emphasis on prediction and control — attitudes that mark the consciousness especially of those of us who are products of twentieth century North American culture. Such lived attitudes that confine the consciousness of the counselor to a merely horizontal world view will confine the consciousness of the counselee as well. This may be acceptable for the counselee whose own sense of life has never gone beyond a certain level, but can be most unhelpful for one who is looking not only for adjustment but for growth and the challenge to become more than he already is.

Even persons who have no pretensions towards growth but who are simply bogged down in daily suffering and neurotic fears, are somehow looking for another whose horizons of meaning are broader than their own, whose life style corresponds somehow to their own sense of how life could and should be. They are looking for one in whom they can have confidence, in whom they can trust. They look for someone with whom they can share not only limitations of the past and hidden fears about the future, but also present weakness and spiritual impoverishment. They look for another who will not remain in a surface relationship, hiding behind his or her functional authority or role as psychologist, helper or counselor, entrenched in ego securities. They look for someone capable of providing a trustworthy place where a troubled person can risk stepping without worrying about being overpowered or dominated. They look, in short, for a human being whose "beneficial presence" points to a horizon of assumptions about life that is beyond either one of them — for a "rainmaker" in whose presence they can blossom.

CHAPTER X

THE CHRISTIAN SPIRITUAL DIRECTOR

Primarily concerned for the Kingdom

It has been understood from the earliest Christian times without exception that guides in the spiritual life should be from among those who had already undergone an initiation into the "Mystery," who had prepared themselves for participation in it, and were already personally knowledgeable about life in the new "way" that the mystery implied. Nevertheless, like the old man in the Chinese legend whose simple, open presence in a dried-up world allowed life-giving rain to fall, contemporary spiritual directors exist with others in a "between-time" world of dryness and drought, in a culture and society that longs for some sort of "rain" in order to blossom forth with new life.

According to Christian revelation, the possibilities for such fruitfulness are not limited to the world's natural condition or confined to effects the world can produce as a result of impulses lying within itself. Its potential immeasurably transcends the world itself.[1] In the time between the Incarnation and the Parousia, our environment as a whole is somehow receptive to the creative will of God directed towards it in what the early Fathers called the time of "the Spirit's dispensation."[2] When Jesus, filled with the Spirit, proclaimed the Good News that the Kingdom of God was at hand, he was revealing to people the incredible fact that the source of life and fruitfulness for all creation was already invisibly present in their very midst. The time of fulfillment, the reign of God, the new creation willed by the Father really was at hand. What was needed were freely receptive and allowing hearts, men and women who believed in and loved the Kingdom, around whom a transformed world, the second creation, could come into being. The Son of God was revealing that the new world would come into being around those who freely became the children of God.

It is the person who has truly undergone a metanoia, and who lives now in the new consciousness of faith, who can be a receptive allowing presence, a portal of entrance into the world for the creative power of God. Such a person, whose basic predispositions are guided by concern for the Kingdom, whose life is increasingly open to the Holy Spirit, is also the one most suited to be a spiritual director of others. It is interesting in this regard to note that for the early Christians, the word "spiritual" did not mean immaterial but meant an effect that was dependent in origin and continuation on the Holy Spirit. The spiritual guide had to be a spiritualized person, one in whom the Holy Spirit lives and acts. Only such an inspirited person can discourse about God and give guidance in the spiritual life.[3] Our human condition as somewhat resistant, unreceptive, narrow and fearful, our basic predisposition to closure and holding on to the status quo, only underlines the need for change, for repentance, for a transformed heart in the one called to be a spiritual guide for others.

The above mentioned interpretation of the word spiritual cuts through another possible misunderstanding as well. The fact that they are engaged in a work having to do primarily with the spiritual dimension, in no way implies that spiritual directors are taken out of or able to bypass all the limiting assumptions of the culture and society of which they too are products. The spiritual directors' presence, like that of every other human being, is inevitably modified by an implicit and often somewhat limiting set of assumptions. They may or may not adhere to any one specific psychological or even philosophical image of the human person, depending on past study in those fields and other factors. Still, each will tend to perceive others in terms of some possibly unacknowledged prereflective image of the human person, to harbor deeply rooted personal and prepersonal intuitions about human liberation and about what fosters and/or hinders or impedes its realization. These unexamined ideas and tendencies may well become obstacles to carrying out the spiritual direction task. However, there is within the historical revelation of Christian tradition, a built in corrective that influences the perception of spiritual directors in that tradition by giving them a revealed image of the human person and his destiny.

Needing a holistic image

Jesus Christ, the prototype of all spiritual directors, came with the message that people were to repent and change their lives because a new creation, a new world of meaning and value, his Kingdom, was at hand. In parables he told about his Father's love for human beings, how the Father had sent him to call everyone to share in a banquet of divine life and love, about the fact that he himself was the Way to that Kingdom. In the Gospels we see him revealing a fresh view of time, of human destiny, the meaning of history, the hidden directionality of the whole world and each person in it. As he gradually brought forward his image of the human person, it became clear that the basis of this image lies in God's love that brought each person into being and fundamentally made each one for a relationship of intimate union with the Father in Christ and through the Holy Spirit. The underlying direction of each person was towards an encounter with Mystery now revealed as three Persons; the hidden direction of the whole of creation was revealed as being towards a state mysteriously called the "new creation." As a matter of fact, throughout the whole of the Judaeo-Christian revelation, the human person had been seen as basically made for relationship, not only with others but also with God. There was a wholeness to the Hebrew mentality that saw man as "presence" not only to partial aspects of creation but also to the mystery of All That Is, to the Creator himself. This view carried over into the Christian understanding of personality in the New Testament as well. The mystery of our divine adoption in Christ revealed by Jesus himself is thus the basis for the possibility of a distinctively Christian image of the human person based on a non-dualistic vision of reality.[4]

We find in the synoptic Gospels an incorporation of this holistic image of the human person implicit in Jesus' description of man in relation to God and others.[5] In Mark's Gospel, when a scribe came up and asked him, "Which is the first of all the commandments?" Jesus replied: "This is the first: Hear, O Israel! The Lord our God is Lord alone! Therefore, you shall love your God with all your heart, with all your soul, with all your mind and with all your strength. This is the second, You shall love your neighbor as yourself." The implicit image underlying these words is a very positive one that assumes a non-dualistic interpenetration of the human person's heart, soul, mind and vital strength in liberating love relationships with self, others and God. Originating as it does in the reality of a transcendent Other as the loving horizon towards which each human being is meant to be directed, this image reveals a new, absolutely original dimension not found in the anthropologies from which most therapeutic counseling emerges. Called by Paul the "pneumatic" or spirit dimension, this new depth refers to that in the human person which permits an encounter with the Pneuma or Holy Spirit of God.[6] It is this spiritual possibility of human participation in the supernatural order that is the primary focus of interest for the spiritual director in the Judaeo-Christian tradition.

The spiritual director's image of the human person must, therefore, include the whole person in terms of the Biblical meaning of the "living soul" in all its potential for relating to the world of vital, psychological and spiritual values that we find variously incorporated in the models that underly the counseling encounter. It is, however, the revealed image of the human person as a pneumatized potential for relating to the persons of the Trinity, for living a graced life that permeates and transforms the vital, psychological and spiritual dimensions of his or her being, that principally informs the perception of the Christian spiritual director.[7]

In our culture at the present moment, this view of the human person in the context of a revealed horizon of faith is rather rare. The lived experience of most people takes place against a taken-for-granted "obvious" ground of psychological or material reality, of governmental, political and social worlds. For men and women today actually to perceive the human person as figure in a ground of spiritual Mystery seems forced, alien and almost pathological. It is difficult for the spiritual director, a product of contemporary culture, who lives in the midst of the relativity of various spiritualities and belief systems, new standards and styles of living, new thought patterns and information overkill, to keep in touch with his or her own experience of the horizon of faith. Yet it is precisely faith in God's revelation of himself in Christ that allows the spiritual director to see human beings as Christ saw them, as capable of loving the Lord their God with their whole heart as well as their whole soul, mind and strength. The heart here refers to the person's original freedom, the secret depths into which the Pneuma of God can come and dwell. The spiritual director's image of the human person focuses on this heart made for relationship, hungry for life, desiring the ultimate. This heart is also far from God. It strays, becomes separated and shut up on itself, grows cold and alienated even from itself. This heart chooses false paths, sets up false gods and ego-functional ways of self-salvation. This heart wants to do right and finds itself doing wrong.[8] It mistakes illusion for reality, denies its own deepest orientation and ends up in sin.

Directors focus on the heart's need for transformation, for metanoia, on its need for mercy and forgiveness, for salvation and humility, for truth and self-acceptance. They are interested more in internal meanings and motivations, in the heart's desire for reconciliation and solidarity with Christ and neighbor. Their image of the human person takes into account a mysterious destiny that cannot be predicted or controlled, a unique initiative from beyond both director and directee that can be discerned as the action of the Holy Spirit "already there" in that heart. Perhaps the major feature of the spiritual directors' image of the human person lies in their knowledge of the heart's freedom to refuse awareness of this transcendent initiative. Directors know that the human person is free to discover and accept this unique entry of the transcendent into the flow of his life, but he is equally free to refuse such entry either because of fear of the unknown, or because of being victimized by a culture that represses spiritual values. Directors who understand the connection of the heart and its freedom to all the manifold dimensions, articulations, modes and modalities of human existence, try to pay attention to both the visible and the invisible, the explicit and the implicit meanings suggested by the more holistic image of the human person as spirit revealed in the Judaeo-Christian tradition.

Lacking a revealed view of the person

Lacking such a basic image of the human person, spiritual directors in the Judaeo-Christian tradition could, and in fact probably would, simply not see the aim of the spiritual direction encounter as helping the person to realize the "already there" dimensions of his own presence as "spirit" or as aiding him in appraisal of the ways in which he might more fully participate in an intimate relationship with the Trinity. Such directors might appreciate the human spirit's capacity to be fascinated and/or awed and frightened by the "more than" in everyday experience, but they would find it difficult to translate this appreciation into concrete directives for a transformation of heart that would be in tune with the unique spiritual destiny this person is called to incarnate in every day living.[9]

The image of the human person that guides the directors' perception must also enable them to distinguish what belongs to the order of the psychical or "spiritual animal" from what belongs to the order of "life-giving spirit," the original dimension of Christian spirituality.[10] They will then be able to avoid much of the current confusion between the two orders that can make even well meaning spiritual directors from the Judaeo-Christian tradition sound more like psychological counselors than like persons with authority and experience in the life of the spirit.

Once aware of the distinctions, they will also be able to make much better use of findings from the psychological disciplines to help untangle the spiritual from all that it is not. For example, the theological virtues of faith, hope and love which make up the foundation of the Christian spiritual life, are not psychological but spiritual — of the order of the Pneuma, not of the psyche. Because they are supernatural they cannot be the object of a psychological analysis. However, a psychological analysis might help to penetrate all that faith is not (the merely affective, sometimes infantile elements and unconscious conflicts surrounding it); or all that hope is not (a merely natural optimism arising from a fortunate temperament); or all that love is not (an isolated affective love or a kind of philanthropy motivated by sentiment or passions).[11] Thus, psychology may clear the way for the real work of spiritual direction. Moreover, a director with a knowledgeable approach to various current psychological models, will be more able, in referral[12] for instance, to make a better choice of therapist, realizing as he or she does that although the model chosen need not actually include any specific spiritual or religious content, it must be open-ended enough that recourse to its techniques does not implicitly promote closure to this dimension of human presence.[13]

Closure to the spiritual order can also come about when persons are caught in a totalization of any one psychological model. This model can actually become for them a substitute for the larger spiritual horizon. It is not surprising that therapists and even spiritual directors in our culture are tempted to absolutize one or the other form of therapy (i.e., expecially those allied to the more spiritual side of man like the Jungian or the phenomenological approaches) until it becomes almost a religious horizon of meaning for them and their directees.[14] Similarly, a strong emphasis on a therapeutic model that does not make room for the spiritual, can have the effect of gradually closing people off from the revealed dimension entirely.[15] So the need to make clear distinctions between the images of the human person appropriate to the psychological counselor and to the spiritual director is emphasized not only bebause there is a difference that must be noted, but also because in actual experience the difference brought about by the inclusion of Revelation, though crucial, is not always immediately recognizeable in practice.

The Practice of disciplined presence

In all great religious traditions, the spiritual guide stands for a vision of reality that is transcendent, that is somehow wider and deeper than his or her own relatively undisciplined and subjective world view. Whether this vision culminates in the mysterious nirvana of Buddhism, in joining the cosmic flow of Taoism, in arriving at the contemplative union of a Sufi mystic, or in being taken up into the Trinitarian mystery of Judaeo-Christian revelation, it carries with it a value system. This value system usually incorporates a way of living, a language and a culture embodying directives and standards that define "the way things are" in objective terms that may or may not fit in with the director's personal thoughts, feelings and momentary whims. Presumably people come to any spiritual guide, teacher, or director because they freely choose to inhabit a deeper life. They wish to be changed in terms of the truth they sense is to be found in the particular vision of reality in which they believe the guide already stands. They desire to integrate the until now scattered fragments of their conflicted selves by following the path or way of living that his more objective vision offers. In this regard, I find similarities between the Eastern and Judaeo-Christian traditions, although in the latter the guide or director does not seem to be as central as does the revealed reality to which he attempts to point.

For Christian spiritual directors, the deeper life or spiritual path is centered in the mystery of Christ as revealed in Scripture and in the Church's traditional teachings, and as it is lived in the history of the people of God.[16] Christian directors in their concern for the Kingdom are always focused beyond the self, on God's plan, on the cosmic significance of Christ, on the world as mysteriously destined for union with God, on the overcoming of alienation by God's salvific initiatives. They are interested and constantly rooting themselves more deeply in the great fundamental mysteries of this divine plan: the incarnation, the redemption, the resurrection, especially as these mysteries can and do permeate the daily processes of inner growth and transformation. Directors must be somewhat consciously aware of the graced "province of meaning"[17] that underlies our matter-of-fact pragmatic existence; they must be able to discern its meanings in and through each person's vital and personal relations to daily events, things and people as well as his or her more specifically spiritual attempts and experiences. Christian directors must be really awake to the "already there" dimension of mystery; they must be willing to surrender their fixed stance in the assumptions of the surrounding culture so as to allow the reality of the resurrection of Jesus to become the horizon in which everyday action and experience is perceived. In the world as people who, though blind, have begun to see the "more than" as gift, as light, as liberation and life for everyone, directors must be "on the way" towards God. As persons who have already said a firm "yes" and entered on the path of continued reawakening to God's initiative in their own life, directors are simply responding to the request for guidance from people who want to travel the same path they themselves are already following.

We can say that the spiritual directors' responsibility with regard to being a disciplined presence for the other is threefold. First of all, they must know the "way," that is, they should have knowledge of the spiritual life and the ways God draws people to himself and communicates his will to them. Foundational spirituality based on the Church's spirituality is centered in scripture, liturgy, sacraments and doctrine as well as on solid reading of universally recognized spiritual masters and authorities. These means are basic if directors are to have an objective knowledge of the spiritual life. Also helpful for spiritual direction is a balanced insight into the principles and findings of the psychology of spirituality and spiritual theology, as long as these are not overestimated or misused.

Secondly, directors must not only know something objective about the life of the Spirit, but they must also have at least begun to live seriously that life themselves, to be "on the way" in listening to the Spirit, in purifying their own hearts and in simplifying their life style so that the task of being sensitive to the Spirit in others will flow from a sensitivity to that Spirit in their own lives. Ultimately, this experience is the source of the directors' perception; it is the origin of their authority to direct, in the sense of pointing to an invisible reality that is more real than the visible appearances seen by physical eyes. In order to avoid being "blind" guides,[18] directors must develop eyes of faith that can discover and appraise the signs of God's presence in the midst of the apparent chaos and complexi-

ty of the directee's everyday life. To see like this, they need
to trust the Spirit of Christ as director for self and others,
and to learn to depend, from personal experience, on the
authority of his love.

Finally, although directors are not meant to attain the
same kind of listening presence as the psychological counselor, there is much that they can learn from this discipline
about the kind of open accepting presence that might be
expected in one whose work involves introducing others to
a basically loving horizon of meaning. Directors should
learn to listen to the other, to develop an attentive presence that is welcoming and positive, free from self preoccupation and artificiality. They also must learn to
reflect on both their own experience and the experience of
the other or of the group, and to communicate these reflections effectively to others. Directors who are just
beginning can profit much from consultation with more
experienced directors who can help them evaluate their
progress. Such persons should have a good understanding
of the relationship of spiritual life and psychic health,
because spiritual direction must respect both creation and
recreation, both nature and grace, and directors ought to
be psychologically as well as spiritually mature enough to
handle (in a loving and free way)[19] the task that has been
given to them.

A mature channel for God's love in the world

Ideally spiritual directors are persons increasingly open
to the Spirit, portals or channels of entrance into the world
for the creative power of God's love. However, they are
also fallible and free to block the channel and misdirect
the life giving flow of grace. A director may refuse to be

the receptive, allowing presence or channel simply by saying a conscious "no" to the Christian vision presented in the Gospel, and by proceeding to *do* spiritual direction as if it were a functional accomplishment achieved by means of the competency of one's own ego-analytical style. Metaphorically, a director who follows this style stunts his or her own growth, and withers spiritually like the branch cut off from Christ.[20] Such a branch cannot bear fruit in isolation from the vine. Similarly cut off, such a director can in reality do nothing, especially in terms of transmission of God's creative life. There is, however, another less conscious way in which the free flow of this life can be blocked. The director embedded in the closed circuit of his or her own personal-vital reactivity, may simply lack the mature freedom to be present to the wider whole. Caught up in the narrow need to be a savior or to impose a particular style of salvation on others, for example, to convert them to a certain spirituality or seduce them by playing on their hidden drives, needs and passions, the psychically immature director can stand in the way of what God would do in others. Paralyzed by his or her own infraconscious hang-ups and hysterical or obsessive needs to be liked, affirmed or seen as perfect; locked into manipulative patterns of competition and achievement; unable to get free of encapsulation in ego modes absorbed from the culture — such a director will be less free to serve those who come for direction.

A mature director, on the contrary, will not seek gratification from directees. He or she will enjoy healthy adult relationships with persons outside the field of the direction task, and will never resort to using directees to fulfill sexual or affective needs. Recognizing the impossibility of totally avoiding the transferential and counter-transferential aspects that inhere in any guidance situation, the mature director will retain a reflective distance from appearances and a frank openness to re-evaluation of every relationship. Aware of personal need for liberation, he or she will value any of life's experiences that bring an increase of interior freedom and detachment. He or she will also welcome opportunities to move out of what might have become an individualistic, privatistic environment into the broader world of social and societal concerns. From a deep involvement in life and its suffering, the mature director will have learned sensitivity and compassion for others who are in pain. Able to perceive them in their transcendent horizon, and liberated from a merely subjective view of reality "as I see it," such a director will be concerned both with what fosters and hinders the person's life of loving union with the Mystery, and also with Christ's command that human beings bear fruit in lives of love for others and thus unconceal the presence of the Kingdom here and now.

In the early Church it was the already baptized Christians who passed on or transmitted the spiritual life of grace to the initiates. The community itself was the spiritual parent that introduced the catechumens to the "way" of Christians — that formed them in values and inner attitudes through communal celebration, personal instruction and direction. Initiates and fully mature Christians together participated in a communal life, one group leading the other on a spiritual path that reached its climax in the celebration of the Paschal Mystery and the birth of new children from the life-giving waters of Baptism. There was no doubt in the minds of these early Christians about Who was the source of this life, about Who was the authority behind everything they said and did in teaching and forming those who asked to be initiated into that life.[21] Each member of the Church was called to be a link between these seekers and the living Other that they sought. Realizing their personal insufficiency for the task, they understood the importance of being channels through which that life of love could flow to those who opened themselves to it. By remaining connected with the Source, by abiding in the living Vine, by being on the Way themselves, these early spiritual directors did not try to *do* the work of transformation on their own. They lived in such a way that they allowed it to be done through them, in somewhat the same way as wire allows an electric current to flow through it.

The spiritual director is basically a limited human being who remains personally in touch with the reality of the Mystery; whose consciousness is permeated by its energy, whose heart is kindled by its love. It is because of this in-touchness with the Real that the spiritual director can be sensitive to all that is not real, that is alien, illusory, untrue. He or she begins with human appearances but moves beneath them to the underlying reality that is their ground, to the guidance of God's Spirit in the person's life.

Spiritual directors in the Christian tradition can be described as actually being channels through whom God's loving plan is allowed to flow into the world, to transform the hearts of men and women in all conditions and states of life. Even if at times their sense of this connectedness disappears or personal and social limitations and sinfulness seem to cut off the flow of grace for a time, mature spiritual directors are aware that their own personal life style can never be the only or even the main influence on those being directed. They are secure in the conviction, belonging to the tradition of the undivided Church, that the Holy Spirit is the primary director and guide, the unfailing companion who leads each person in his or her own unique way. St. John of the Cross also maintains that spiritual directors are not the chief agents or movers of souls. The principle guide is the Holy Spirit who, he says, is never neglectful. Directors, who must learn to observe well the road along which God is leading their directees, are merely, according to him, the instruments God uses to direct people to Him through faith and observance of his law.[22] Thus we return to Christ, whose Spirit is *the* spiritual guide, the living context, the source of life for everyone. Christ, the one who has already saved and redeemed, is the spiritual master who ultimately loves, directs and is responsible for both the director and those directed. What we need to learn is to be present prayerfully to what is already there — to the Trinitarian Mystery that is of all possible spiritual direction, both the goal and the Way.

FOOTNOTES

CHAPTER I

INTRODUCTION

1. John T. McNeill, *A History of the Cure of Souls* (New York: Harper and Row, 1977), p. vii.

2. See McNeill, op. cit. for an excellent bibliography on the history of guidance from the wise men of ancient Israel and the Greek philosophers to contemporary psychiatrists and Christian counselors. Also Kenneth Leech, *Soul Friend; a Study of Spirituality* (London: Sheldon Press, 1977).

CHAPTER II

EARLIEST CHRISTIAN SPIRITUAL DIRECTION

1. Mk. 1:9. All scriptural quotations, unless otherwise noted, are taken from *The New American Bible* (New York: P.J. Kenedy and Sons, 1970).

2. Stephen Verney, *Into the New Age* (Glasgow: Collins, 1976), p. 45.

3. Mt. 13:9, 43.

4. See Mt. 13, Mk. 4.

5. Mt. 16:13-15.

6. Mt. 16:16.

7. Mk. 10:17-25.

8. Mk. 10:21-22.

9. Lk. 19.

10. See *The Interpreter's Bible* (New York: Abingdon, 1952), p. 321.

11. Lk. 19:9-10.

12. Mk. 5:18-20.

13. Mk. 7:26.

14. Mt. 8:10, Lk. 7:9.

15. Eph. 3:3.

16. Mt. 13:11-18.

17. The phrase "undivided church" refers to the universal revealed tradition held by the great spiritual masters before the division between East and West. See Aelred Squire, *Asking the Fathers* (New York: Paulist Press, 1973).

18. Rom. 8:19.

19. See *Rite of Christian Initiation of Adults* (Washington, D.C.: United States Catholic Conference, 1974) plus commentaries on early church baptismal rites.

20. Lk. 24.

21. Acts 2, cf. Acts 10.

22. Acts 2:32-33.

23. Ibid.

24. cf. Rom. 7, 8 and Gal. 5.

25. Rom. 8:11.

26. See Adrian van Kaam, *On Being Yourself* (Denville, N.J.: Dimension Books, 1972) for an introduction to the self-theory underlying this description.

27. Rom. 8:14-16.

28. 2 Cor. 3:17.

29. 2 Cor. 3:18.

30. See George A. Maloney, *Man — the Divine Icon* (Pecos, N.M.: Dove Publications, 1973).

31. 2 Cor. 4:18.

32. Rom. 5:2.

33. See especially Rom. 6.

34. Rom. 7:15.

35. Rom. 7:16.

36. Rom. 7:24-25.

37. 1 Cor. 2:7-9.

38. 1 Cor. 2:10.

39. 1 Cor. 2:12.

40. 1 Cor. 2:14.

41. 1 Jn. 3:1-2.

42. Jn. 4:14; Jn. 7:38.

43. Mk. 4:27.

44. Eph. 1:10.

45. 1 Cor. 2:10.

46. This section is based on the article "The Spiritual Father in Orthodox Christianity" by Kallistos Ware. *Cross Currents,* Summer/Fall, 1974, pp. 296-313.

47. In Anthony's life also we find a preparation in the desert; his being chosen as spiritual guide by the people; knowledge and revelation of a hidden mystery via a dialogual method and the practice of adding particular guidance to the general instructions for everyone.

48. Kallistos Ware in the article described above.

49. Lk. 10:42.

50. Jn. 1:38-42.

51. Lk. 3:10-18.

CHAPTER III

THE STRUCTURE OF GUIDANCE SITUATIONS

1. Mk. 10:17-25; Jn. 6:25-59.

2. For an introductory description of lived worlds of meaning, see John Macquarrie, *Paths in Spirituality* (New York: Harper and Row, 1972).

3. This way of perceiving any experience as a gestalt of figure on a ground, as a visible constellation of related elements emerging from an invisible "already there" context can be useful for sorting out the meaning of a variety of different life experiences.

4. The phrase "neuroses are socioses" is from an article entitled "What is psychotherapy" by J.H. Van den Berg, *Humanitas,* 1971, 7(3), pp. 321-370. See also his *Divided Existence and Complex Society* (New Jersey: Humanities Press, 1974).

5. Whether it becomes "spiritual guidance" is very much influenced by the values that can be lived in the society itself and their possibility for expression in the lives of the persons themselves.

6. This discussion of the various "self" levels is based on the self-theory of Van Kaam as exemplified in his *The Dynamics of Spiritual Self-Direction* (Denville, N.J.: Dimension Books, 1976).

7. Refers to man's substitutions of a safe, controllable beyond for the Great Beyond, as in Ernest Becker's *The Denial of Death* (New York: The Free Press, 1973) and in *Escape from Evil* (New York: The Free Press, 1975).

8. See R.D. Laing, *The Divided Self* (Baltimore, Md.: Penguin Books, 1965) and Van den Berg, op. cit.

9. See Adrian van Kaam, *The Transcendent Self* (Denville, N.J.: Dimension Books, 1979).

10. References to the ego and its necessary moments of power-lessness or desparation can be found in a chapter on "The Nature of the Ego and its Termination" in Meher Baba, *Discourses* (3. vol. San Francisco: Sufism Reoriented Inc., 1976).

11. One way of expressing   "The problem that has no name" is Betty Frieden's *The Feminine Mystique* (New York: Dell Publishing, 1963).

CHAPTER IV

WHAT SPIRITUAL DIRECTION IS NOT

1. The West's forgetfulness of the fundamental instrumental or practical nature of religious forms is mentioned in the introduction to Jacob Needleman's, *The New Religions* (New York: Doubleday, 1970).

2. However, he or she must also be aware that the dynamics of Christian spiritual direction can sometimes be in opposition to what our culture accepts as human liberation. See last section of Chapter VI for illustration.

3. See Chapter VII, "The particular individual who comes," for more on the inextricable relatedness of the person and his or her world.

4. For example, a person could seek out a medical doctor for help with a physical illness, but the doctor must be clear about the limits of his or her medical skill if the illness seems to have a psychological origin and/or ethical, situational or spiritual implications. In the same vein, a spiritual director must be clear about his or her limitations as regards psychological, moral, ethical or confessional matters, since many encounters will encompass all of these dimensions.

5. Hilde Bruch, *Learning Psychotherapy* (Cambridge, Mass.: Harvard University Press, 1974), p. ix.

6. Ibid.

7. Ibid.

8. See "Tyranny of the should" in Karen Horney's, *Neurosis and Human Growth* (New York: W.W. Norton, 1950).

9. Not only individuals, but whole societies as well may be more or less oriented towards a view of reality that transcends the apparent satisfactions afforded by the "givens" of their particular culture.

10. In a chapter on "Introspection and Transcendent Self-presence" in *In Search of Spiritual Identity* (Denville, N.J.: Dimension Books, 1975), Adrian van Kaam points to transcendent self-presence as a condition for the emergence of this meaning.

11. See footnote 25, Chapter VII, on "transference".

12. Much of the discussion on the pastoral counseling movement is based on Leech's Chapter Three in *Soul Friend* (London: Sheldon Press, 1977).

13. Ibid.

CHAPTER V

A NATURAL FOUNDATION FOR SPIRITUAL DIRECTION

1. For further references to the natural human capacity for mystical experience see Annie Dillard, *Pilgrim at Tinker Creek* (New York: Bantam Books, 1974); Karlfried von Durkheim, *The Way of Transformation* (Winchester, MA.: Allen and Unwin, 1971); Margaret Furse, *Mysticism; Window on a World View* (Nashville, Tenn.: Abingdon Press, 1977); F.C. Happold, *Mysticism* (Harmondsworth: Penguin, 1963); Lawrence LeShan, *Alternate Realities* (New York: M. Evans, 1976); Evelyn Underhill, *Practical Mysticism* (New York: E.P. Dutton, 1915).

2. Abraham Maslow, *Religions, Values and Peak-experiences* (New York: Viking, 1964).

3. Thomas Aquinas, *Summa Theologiae,* part 1, Q1, art. 2, ad. 2.

4. Freud's rather unspiritual dictum, "where id is should ego be," an expression of purpose that caused Jung to break with him because he could "find no room, no breathing space in the constricting atmosphere of Freudian psychology and its narrow outlook," is finding a similar lack of acceptance among contemporary clients who, although they may not want a restructuration of consciousness in the context of any special revelation, do need and want, by means of reflection on experience, to restructure their conscious presence to somehow include the "more" of reality that has so far seemed to elude them. J. Campbell (Ed.), *The Portable Jung* (New York: 1971), p. xx-xxi.

5. The reader may be acquainted with *The Journal of Transpersonal Psychology,* or with Charles Tart (Ed.), *Transpersonal Psychologies* (New York: Harper and Row, 1975) both of which point to increased interest on the part of psychologists in the transcendent dimension. Several years ago, in a speech devoted to trying to sort through the contemporary tangle of psychiatry and spirituality, Jacob Needleman remarked that the line is blurred that divides the therapist from the spiritual guide. As one observer put it: "The shrinks are beginning to sound like gurus, and the gurus are beginning to sound like shrinks." See "Psychiatry and the Sacred" in Jacob Needleman (Ed.), *On the Way to Self-knowledge* (New York: Knopf, 1976).

6. In the above-mentioned article, Needleman's observation that psychiatry seems to be replacing the religious institutions of the West in dealing with questions of personal identity and ultimate meaning seems to touch on a major problematic area for the Christian spiritual director, who, while freely disavowing any identity as either "guru" or "shrink," finds himself subtly pressured into attempting, usually ineptly, to fill the role of

therapist, theologically-oriented counselor or even Freudian wise man from the East.

7. For further discussion of the possibility that reality has of presenting itself as partial wholes as well as one undivided unity of All That Is, and the complimentary possibility that the human person (and/or scientist) has of being present to reality either totally or with openness only on one level, see Adrian van Kaam, *Existential Foundations of Psychology* (New York: Doubleday, 1969). The possibility of what he calls "differential theoretical modes of existence" in psychology accounts for much of the contemporary confusion that accompanies the whole question of the legitimate areas aimed at in the various types of counseling therapy.

8. Abraham Maslow, "Lessons from the peak-experience," *Journal of Humanistic Psychology,* 1961, 2(12).

9. Such seeing is thematic in Thomas Hora's *Existential Metapsychiatry* (New York: Seabury Press, 1977) and also in his *Dialogues in Metapsychiatry* (New York: Seabury Press, 1977), for example.

10. Use here of the adjective "natural" is meant to characterize this thinking as belonging to the "natural attitude" — a phrase used by Alfred Schutz in his *Collected Papers* (The Hague: Nijhoff, 1967) and described further in Chapter VII, footnote 9, of this book.

11. One such therapy is "metapsychiatry" as found in Thomas Hora, op. cit.

12. The notion of finite provinces of meaning is prominent in the thinking of William James, *Principles of Psychology* (11, New York: Dover Publications, 1950) and Alfred Schutz, *Collected Papers,* op. cit., Chapter on "On multiple realities." Also, under the influence of the Taoist approach to "wider consciousness," therapists are not only discovering how the patient avoids, blocks and distorts his sensory, expressive, intentional presence to the immediate experience of visible people, events and things, but they are increasingly interested in how patients

can open themselves to the larger invisible "flow" or unifying ground from which those people, events and things emerge.

13. A few examples of literature available on the subject: Patricia Carrington, *Freedom in Meditation* (New York: Doubleday, 1977); Jean-Marie Dechanet, *Christian Yoga* (New York: Harper, 1956); William Johnston, *Silent Music* (London: Fontana, 1974); Lawrence LeShan, *How to Meditate* (New York: Bantam Books, 1974); Claudio Naranjo, *The One Quest* (London: Wildwood House, 1972); Claudio Naranjo and Robert Ornstein, *On the Psychology of Meditation* (New York: Viking, 1961); Adam Smith, *Powers of the Mind* (Westminster, Md.: Random House, 1975); Charles Tart, *Transpersonal Psychologies* (Scranton, Pa.: Harper and Row, 1975).

14. Jacob Needleman, *The New Religions* (New York: Doubleday, 1970), p. 17.

15. The S-R or stimulus-response paradigm indicates the basic structure of the behavioral theory of personality — a closed circuit of reaction to stimuli in which persons without the power to break that circuit by means of reflection and decision are condemned to dwell. Again the reader is referred to Adrian van Kaam, *In Search of Spiritual Identity,* op. cit., Chapter VII.

16. One of the most highly regarded of the guides to meditation is Patricia Carrington's, *Freedom in Meditation,* op. cit.

17. For further discussion of this point, see William Johnston, *Silent Music; the Science of Meditation* (New York: Harper and Row, 1974), especially Chapter 3, "Brainwave and Biofeedback."

18. All scripture quotations in this section only are taken from *The Jerusalem Bible* (New York: Doubleday, 1966). After the address and greeting, the first chapter of Paul's Letter to the Church at Ephesus bears the subhead "The Mystery of Salvation and of the Church," God's plan of salvation.

19. Eph. 4:17-18, Eph. 2.

20. Eph. 5:10-14.

21. Eph. 4:23.

22. Eph. 1:18-19.

23. Eph. 2:1-5.

24. Eph. 3:7. Actually it is the subhead that designated Paul as servant of the Mystery.

25. Eph. 3:16-19.

26. The reader is referred to the incarnational theory of the human person embodied in van Kaam's *In Search of Spiritual Identity* (op. cit.), particularly Chapters V and VI.

27. Eph. 3:20.

CHAPTER VI

SPIRITUAL DIRECTION OF CHRISTIANS

1. In imitation of John the Baptist whose spiritual direction of the people was based on the belief that "He (Christ) must increase while I must decrease," (Jn. 3:30).

2. Thomas Aquinas, *Summa Theologiae,* part 2, Q 68, art. 2.

3. "Direction can be defined as the help one man gives to another to enable him to become himself in his faith," Jean LaPlace, *Preparing for Spiritual Direction* (Chicago: Franciscan Herald Press, 1975), p. 26. "Spiritual direction is the continuous process of formation and guidance in which a Christian is led and encouraged in his or her special vocation, so that by faithful correspondence to the graces of the Holy Spirit, he may attain to the particular end of his vocation and to union with God," Thomas Merton, *Spiritual Direction and Meditation* (Collegeville, Minn.: Liturgical Press, 1959), p. 5. "The end of spiritual direction is to aid a person to know the plan of God for his life and to put into practice daily the resources which God has given for the realization of this plan," *Dictionnaire de Spiritualite* (Paris: Beauchesne, 1957), p. 1143.

4. This transition appears almost 100 times in the Gospel of St. John where the life of faith is likened to seeing, and Cornelius Ernst, in *The Theology of Grace* (Notre Dame. Ind.: Fides, 1973) compares the life of grace to a new perception of reality. Cf. also Romano Guardini, "The Blind and the Seeing" in *The Lord* (Chicago: Regnery, 1954).

5. Acts 9:1-19; Acts 22:5-16; Acts 26:10-18: Ga. 1:12-17.

6. See Adrian van Kaam, *In Search of Spiritual Identity* (Denville, N.J.: Dimension Press, 1975), Chapter 5, for dimensions of human spiritual presence in terms of fields of consciousness.

7. Louis Bouyer, in the first chapter of his *Introduction to Spirituality* (New York: Desclee, 1961) points to the error of "psychologism," the tendency to reduce the spiritual life to certain states of consciousness.

8. See Léon Dufour, *Dictionary of Biblical Theology* (New York: Seabury Press, 1973), pp. 228-229 for meaning of the term "heart" in the Old and New Testaments. Also see Stephen Strasser, *Phenomenology of Feeling* (Pittsburgh: Duquesne University Press, 1977) for a phenomenological approach to the human heart.

9. 1 Cor. 2:10-16.

10. Many literary and psycho-spiritual works speak of everyday experiences which evoke a response to the "more then." See for example Andrew Greely, *Ecstasy; a Way of Knowing* (Englewood Cliffs, N.J.: Prentice-Hall, 1974); Annie Dillard, *Pilgrim at Tinker Creek* (New York: Bantam Books, 1974); William James, *Varieties of Religious Experience* (New York: New American Library, 1958).

11. Jacques Ellul, *The Technological Society* (New York: Vintage Books, 1964) was one of the first to analyze our technical civilization and its effect on the persons in it. The term "technological trance" was used in a public lecture by Thomas Berry at Grailville, Loveland, Ohio, Dec. 1976.

12. Just as in the field of music there are geniuses like Mozart

whose reports of what they hear are believed by the less gifted and literally heard by those more sensitive to sound, so in the religious dimension, there are geniuses like the great mystics whose reports of the Way Things Are are believed by those less gifted with sensitivity to signals of transcendence.

13. Eph. 1:9.

14. Adrian van Kaam, op. cit., especially Chapter VI.

15. Ex. 3:14.

16. Jn. 15:1-8.

17. Ernest Becker, *Denial of Death* (New York: The Free Press, 1973), Chapter IV, speaks of anxiety in reaction to global helplessness which from early childhood may evoke a system of defences in young human beings. All humans, in attempting to deny this anxiety, develop a defensive character armor and substitute worlds of drivenness in which to hide from the call to be who they most truly are that comes from the Great Beyond.

18. Thomas Merton, *The New Man* (New York: New American Library, 1961), p. 45-46.

19. See Adrian van Kaam, *The Dynamics of Spiritual Self Direction* (Denville, N.J.: Dimension Books, 1976), Chapter 14, on the differences between spiritual and psychological direction.

CHAPTER VII

THE PARTICULAR INDIVIDUAL WHO COMES

1. Some spiritual directors with little phenomenological or psychological background may find the concepts and language of this chapter somewhat unfamiliar. However, it is for the sake of the people who tend to describe their spiritual needs in terms of more philosophical or psychological concepts and language that directors need to widen their own horizons in the direction of the human sciences.

2. This chapter will not deal at all with the psychotic person.

3. For an overview of the history of this philosophical movement, see Herbert Spiegelberg, *The Phenomenological Movement* (The Hague: Nijhoff, 1969, 2.v.) For an overview of its impact on the field of psychology, see Hendryk Misiak, *Phenomenological, Existential and Humanistic Psychologies* (New York: Grune and Stratton, 1971). Adrian van Kaam is the only theorist who articulates this view in terms of a contemporary Christian image of the human person as fundamentally spirit.

4. In an essay on "What is psychotherapy" *Humanitas,* 1971, 7(3), pp. 321-370, J.H. Van den Berg points to spirituality as the sector of social life presently being repressed or "pushed into the unconscious." In like manner, van Kaam in a chapter on "Obstacles to religious presence" *Personality Fulfillment in the Spiritual Life* (Wilkes-Barre, Pa.: Dimension Books, 1966) points to the repression or denial of the sacred dimension, one of the essential modes of being.

5. For a general phenomenological insight into the meaning of "situatedness" the reader may consult the works of Maurice Merleau-Ponty, and especially *Phenomenology of Perception* (New York: Humanities Press, 1962) where he notes that the central phenomenon at the root of both my subjectivity and my transcendence towards others consists in . . . (the fact that) I find myself already situated and involved in a physical and social world.

6. See William Luijpen, *Existential Phenomenology* (Pittsburgh, Pa.: Duquesne University Press, 1969) particularly Chapter 3, "Phenomenology of Freedom."

7. See Chapter VI, section on "Connection of baptism with mission" for the importance of discovering one's unique spiritual identity or direction.

8. For more on the life style known as character armor, see Ernest Becker's *Angel in Armor* (Macmillan: The Free Press, 1969).

9. A description of life lived in the "natural attitude" is given by Alfred Schutz, *Collected Papers* (The Hague: Nijhoff, 1967), pp. 105-107. It is a pragmatic attitude that assumes the world could not be otherwise than as it appears to us in the world of daily life, (p. 209).

10. For typical periodic crises see Gail Sheehy, *Passages* (New York: Bantam, 1977); Adrian van Kaam, *The Transcendent Self* (Denville, N.J.: Dimension Books, 1979); Daniel Levinson, *Seasons of a Man's Life* (New York: Knopf, 1978).

11. Adrian van Kaam, *In Search of Spiritual Identity* (Denville, N.J.: Dimension Books, 1975), p. 143.

12. See Maurice Merleau-Ponty, op. cit., p. 410-433, where the author describes the person as a perceptual field drawing along a wake of retentions from the past while biting into the future with its protentions.

13. Limit or boundary situations are defined by Karl Jaspers as situations that go with existence itself. They are like a wall we run into, a wall on which we founder . . . they never change, except in appearance. *Philosophy, Vol. II* (Chicago: University of Chicago Press, 1970), p. 178.

14. Adrian van Kaam, op. cit., pp. 172-196.

15. Karen Horney, op. cit., (Footnote 8, Chapter IV).

16. Adrian van Kaam. From a gestalt point of view, partial aspects of All That Is such as one's family, one's work, one's health, one's recreation can and often do become the whole — the substitute in one's life for the horizon of All That Is.

17. These descriptions of totalized intermediate wholes were given in lectures at Duquesne University in Pittsburgh at the Institute of Formative Spirituality by Adrian van Kaam.

18. The phrase "normal madness" is from the thought of R.D. Laing in his books *The Divided Self; An Existential Study in Sanity and Madness* (Chicago: Quadrangle Books, 1960); *The Self and Others* (Chicago: Quadrangle Books, 1962) and *The Politics of Experience* (New York: Pantheon Books, 1967).

19. Psychiatrists like Adler, Horney, Sullivan, Fromm, Erikson and Van den Berg as well as the members of the Human Potential Movement, the transactionalists and gestaltists and other humanistically oriented practitioners are referred to here.

20. Defined by its originator as being the person's wish to be in harmony with a unit he or she regards as extending beyond his individual self, homonomy is seen to be a powerful motivating source of behavior. See Andras Angyal, "The trend towards homonomy" in *Neurosis and Treatment* (New York: Viking, 1965).

21. An overview of such literature is provided in Frank Johnston's *Alienation; Concept, Term and Meaning* (New York: Seminar Press, 1973).

22. An expression used by Bruno Bettelheim to describe the defended self of the schizophrenic person. *The Empty Fortress* (New York: Free Press, 1967).

23. Theorists like Fromm, Laing, Kardiner, Coles, etc. see socio-economic factors as a major link in the etiology of mental illness.

24. Ernest Becker, *Escape from Evil* (New York: The Free Press, 1975), p. 127, goes beyond the classic Freudian meaning of transference to explain in the last part of his book how transference seen as a necessary projection of the meaning of life beyond oneself can be one way of taking care of the overwhelmingness of the universe. He also has a chapter on transference in the sense of the temptation to make a "god" of another human being in his book *The Denial of Death* (New York: The Free Press, 1973).

25. Many contemporary therapists see the classic perception of transference as a distortion of the encounter between two human beings. Commenting on the phenomenological bases of psychotherapy, Rollo May notes ". . . we have all kinds of studies of transference . . . which tell us everything except what really goes on between two human beings." In E.E. Straus,

(Ed.), *Phenomenology: Pure and Applied* (Pittsburgh: Duquesne University Press, 1964).

26. Karen Horney, *Neurosis and Human Growth* (New York: W.W. Norton, 1950). The three typical coping patterns are grouped by Horney under the appeals of mastery, love and freedom. The expansive solution to relieve neurotic tension is lived out by the aggressive type; the self-effacing solution by the compliant type and resignation by the detached type. The following paragraphs, because of their brevity, are necessarily somewhat of a caricature of her typologies which should be studied in the original.

27. Of the three "solutions," this one seems most attractive in our competitive culture, to judge simply from the number of books on the shelves about being a success, looking out for #1, being assertive, being born to win, etc.

CHAPTER VIII

THE PERSON FROM A SPIRITUAL POINT OF VIEW

1. See especially Gal. 5 and Rm. 8.

2. Cornelius Ernst, *The Theology of Grace* (Notre Dame, Ind.: Fides, 1973).

3. Ga. 5:13-17.

4. "Ontos," the Greek word for "being," is at the root of ontological as descriptive of the anxiety that reaches to the fundamental structures of human existence. It is an anxiety that arises from the stark awareness of simply being thrown into the infinite universe — an anxiety captured in Pascal's "The eternal silence of these infinite spaces frightens me," *Pascal's Pensées* (New York: Dutton, 1958), p. 61. See also Paul Tillich, *The Courage to Be* (New Haven: Yale University Press, 1952).

5. Acts 17.

6. See Jean LaPlace, *Preparing for Spiritual Direction* (Chicago: Franciscan Herald Press, 1975).

7. This opinion in no way discounts the "conversion" power of cosmic consciousness experiences and the opening that such jolts in perception may give to alternate realities on many different levels of meaning.

8. See Chapter VI, footnote 8.

9. See Adrian van Kaam, *The Transcendent Self; The Formative Spirituality of Middle, Early and Later Years of Life* (Denville, N.J.: DImension Books, 1979) for a more detailed account of the various phases and periods encountered by the self.

10. See Adrian van Kaam, "Psychic Health and Spiritual Life," *New Catholic World,* 1976, Mar./Apr., pp. 75-79.

11. The reader is referred to a forthcoming publication of Adrian van Kaam tentatively titled *The Science of Formative Spirituality* which will embody the unified formation theory that underlies this vision of the emerging self. See also *Dynamics of Spiritual Self Direction,* pp. 13-14.

12. Eph. 4:23 (Jerusalem Bible)

13. Van Kaam, ibid., pp. 14-16.

14. See John Hoffman, *Practical Union with God* (New York: Catholic Book Publishing Co., 1949), pp. 133-137 for examples of sinful modes rooted in nature or individual character.

15. Adrian van Kaam, ibid., pp. 20-27.

16. Ibid., Chapter 4, "Guilt and self-direction."

17. Spiritual direction in any of the other great religious traditions of mankind would be described within a different context, but a similar necessary structure of the direction always emerges. In each we find a figure (the particular tradition) that receives its meaning in relation to a larger horizon (the Sacred).

18. It is of course not absolutely necessary that a person be baptized before seeking spiritual direction in a Christian context.

19. Cf. 1 Thes. 5:23 — a blessing that takes wholeness for granted.

20. See Chapter X for a holistic biblical image of the human person centered in the heart.

21. Aelred Squire writes in his chapter "In the Land of Unlikeness" that sin gets its meaning from our sublime destiny as sharers in God's life. We have lost a dynamic wholeness that we can see could and should be ours. Sin is failing to measure up to what should be; a situation of disharmony in which we find ourselves. *Asking the Fathers* (New York: Paulist Press, 1973).

22. In Gal. 5:15-25, Paul speaks of the values of the "flesh" as opposed to those of the "spirit," of the conflict between the old and the new orders. Christians do not find real freedom in giving rein to cravings for values that direct them away from their relationship to Christ.

23. Julian of Norwich, *Revelations of Divine Love* (New York: Doubleday, 1977), p. 178. "I saw that God never started loving mankind. For the condition man shall have in endless bliss, completely filling up the joy of God as far as his works are concerned, shall be exactly the same as that he has had in the foresight of God — known and loved from without beginning in God's rightful intent."

24. In contrast to psychological counselling that has traditionally dealt mainly with fixations from the past.

25. Adrian van Kaam, ibid., Chapters 8-10.

26. There are parallels in Eastern spiritual direction with St. Paul's advice to the Ephesians to "lay aside your former way of life and old self which deteriorates through illusion and desire and acquire a fresh spiritual way of thinking." Eph. 4:22.

27. As in J.B. Phillips, *Your God is Too Small* (New York: Macmillan, 1974) and Malachi Martin, *Jesus Now* (Toronto: Popular Library, 1973).

28. See Chapter III, footnote 7.

29. As seen earlier, it is possible to make a "religion" of devotion to lesser beyonds of family, work, social action, politics, the arts, science, therapy, friendship, power, possessions, etc.

30. See Chapter VII, footnote 9.

31. For an understanding of this term in its Eastern sense, see Chogyam Trungpa, *Cutting Through Spiritual Materialism* (Berkely: Shambala, 1973).

32. For a further development of the three relational typologies of neurotic compliance, aggression and detachment, see Samuel I. Greenberg, *Neurosis is a Painful Style of Living* (New York: New American Library, 1971).

33. See Adrian van Kaam, "Obstacles to Religious Presence" in his *Personality Fulfillment in the Spiritual Life* (Wilkes-Barre, Pa.: Dimension Books, 1966).

34. Acts 17:28.

35. Gal. 5:22-23.

CHAPTER IX

PRESENCE OF THE THERAPIST

1. Irene de Castillejo, *Knowing Women* (New York: Harper and Row, 1973) Chapter 9. Jolande Jacobi, *Masks of the Soul* (Grand Rapids, Mich.: Eerdmans, 1976), Chapter 1.

2. Thomas Hora, *Existential Metapsychiatry* (New York: Seabury Press, 1977), p. 42.

3. Depends on one's underlying view of the human person as totally determined (positivistic) or as totally free (idealistic).

4. Anthony Barton, *Three Worlds of Therapy* (Palo Alto; Ca.: National Press Books, 1974), Chapter II.

5. Adrian van Kaam, *In Search of Spiritual Identity* (Denville, N.J.: Dimension Books, 1975), Chapter 5.

6. Adrian van Kaam, *The Art of Existential Counseling* (Wilkes-Barre, Pa.: Dimension Books, 1966), where the influence of the author's personality theory is particularly evident in Chapters 6 and 7.

7. See Anthony Barton, op. cit. regarding therapist's values.

8. Thomas Hora, op. cit.

9. See Chapter VII, footnote 25.

10. In his analysis of the therapist as bearer of value, Barton (op. cit.) exposes nondirectiveness as an impossibility in view of the inevitability of co-constitution.

11. See Eugene Kennedy, *On Becoming a Counselor* (New York: Seabury Press, 1977), Chapter 17 for signs of counter-transferential reaction in the counselor.

CHAPTER X

THE CHRISTIAN SPIRITUAL DIRECTOR

1. This point of the *potentia obedientalis* of the world is explained in the chapter on "Providence" in Romano Guardini's *The World and the Person* (Chicago: Regnery, 1965).

2. Adrian Nocent, *The Liturgical Year,* vol. 1 (Collegeville, Minn.: Liturgical Press, 1977), p. 39.

3. George Maloney, *The Breath of the Mystic* (Denville, N.J.: Dimension Books, 1974), p. 119-120.

4. Aelred Squire, *Asking the Fathers* (New York: Paulist Press, 1973) Chapter 2; Joseph Fichtner, *Man, the Image of God* (New York: Alba House, 1978); George Maloney, *Man — the Divine Icon* (Pecos, N.M.: Dove Publications, 1973).

5. Mk. 12:28-34; Mt. 22:34-40; Lk. 10:25-28: cf. Dt. 6:4-5.

6. Claude Tresmontant, *A Study of Hebrew Thought* (New York: Desclee, 1960), especially Part II, "An Outline of Biblical Anthropology."

7. The reader is referred to Chapter 2 for the first description of the aim of spiritual direction.

8. Rom. 7:19.

9. Adrian van Kaam, *In Search of Spiritual Identity* (Denville, N.J.: Dimension Books, 1975), Chapter V on "Spiritual Identity and Modes of Incarnation."

10. Tresmontant, op. cit,. pp. 87-114.

11. Ibid., p. 113.

12. Eugene Kennedy, *On Becoming a Counselor* (New York: Seabury Press, 1977), Chapter 17 on "The Problem of Referral."

13. See Chapter IX, section on counselor's ways of evoking the other.

14. At one time this absolutizing of one form of therapy, e.g. the Rogerian model, did happen for a great many clergymen of all denominations.

15. E.F. O'Doherty, *Religion and Psychology* (New York: Alba House, 1978), Chapter I, "Freud and Jung," provides an interesting discussion of this question.

16. Spiritual theology, scripture, the writing of the Fathers, theologians and spiritual masters are frequently most directly relevant to the inner life of the Christian. See Susan Muto, *A Practical Guide to Spiritual Reading* (Denville, N.J.: Dimension Books, 1976).

17. See Chapter V, footnote 12.

18. St. John of the Cross, *The Living Flame of Love,* Chapter III, pp. 29, 30, and 31. In *The Collected Works of St. John of the Cross* (Washington, D.C.: Institute of Carmelite Studies, 1973).

19. Thus, it is recommended that spiritual directors become familiar with the ordinary ways in which therapists discipline themselves in loving availability, to let go of their own self-preoccupation for example, in order to give full attention to

their clients.

20. Jn. 15:5.

21. *The Rite of Christian Initiation of Adults* (Washington, D.C.: United States Catholic Conference, 1974).

22. St. John of the Cross, op. cit., Chapter III, p. 46.